Aquatic Life
of the World

Volume 2
Bass–Conservation

Marshall Cavendish Corporation
99 White Plains Road
Tarrytown, New York 10591–9001

© 2001 Marshall Cavendish Corporation

Library of Congress Cataloging-in-Publication Data
Aquatic life of the world.
    p.   cm.
    Contents: v. 1. Abalone–Barracuda — v. 2. Bass–Conservation — v. 3. Continental shelf–Fiddler crab — v. 4. Fin whale–Hydrothermal vent — v. 5. Iceberg–Manatee and dugong — v. 6. Mangrove–Ocean history — v. 7. Oceanography–Puffin — v. 8. Remora–Sea otter — v. 9. Sea pen–Swordfish — v. 10. Tarpon–Wrasse — v. 11. Index.
    ISBN 0-7614-7170-7 (set) — ISBN 0-7614-7171-5 (v. 1) — ISBN 0-7614-7172-3 (v. 2) — ISBN 0-7614-7173-1 (v. 3) — ISBN 0-7614-7174-X (v. 4) — ISBN 0-7614-7175-8 (v. 5) — ISBN 0-7614-7176-6 (v. 6) — ISBN 0-7614-7177-4 (v. 7) — ISBN 0-7614-7178-2 (v. 8) — ISBN 0-7614-7179-0 (v. 9) — ISBN 0-7614-7180-4 (v. 10) — ISBN 0-7614-7181-2 (index)
    1. Aquatic biology—Juvenile literature. [1. Aquatic biology—Encyclopedias. 2. Marine animals—Encyclopedias. 3. Freshwater animals—Encyclopedias.] I. Marshall Cavendish Corporation.

QH90.16.A78 2000
578.76—dc21

99-086128

ISBN 0-7614-7170-7 (set)
ISBN 0-7614-7172-3 (volume 2)

Printed in Hong Kong

06 05 04 03 02 01   6 5 4 3 2 1

Brown Partworks
Project editor: Bridget Giles
Subeditors: Amanda Harman, Tim Harris, Tom Jackson, James Kinchen, Jane Scarsbrook, Jens Thomas
Managing editor: Anne O'Daly
Designer: Alison Gardner
Picture researchers: Veneta Bullen, Helen Simm
Illustrator: Christopher Jory
Graphics: Mark Walker
Indexer: Kay Ollerenshaw

Marshall Cavendish Corporation
Editor: Marian Armstrong
Editorial director: Paul Bernabeo

WRITERS

Richard Beatty
Dylan Bright
Jen Green
James Kinchen
Dr. Robbie A. MacDonald
Samantha Rohr

Paul L. Sieswerda
Dr. Sergio Steffani
Dr. Robert Stewart
Dr. Robert Stickney
Dr. Laurence G. Riddle
Brian Ward

CONTENTS

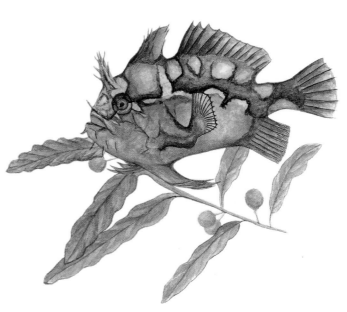

BASS

◀ A Florida large-mouth black bass lurks in wait for some likely prey to swim by.

Bass are large, aggressive fish native to the freshwaters of North America. Their eagerness to strike a lure and hard-fighting qualities when hooked have made them a favorite target for fishers. Large members of the sunfish family, bass are important predators in many rivers and lakes across the United States.

BASS BASICS

With a compact, heavy build and large jaws, a bass can easily accelerate forward and seize prey. Sharp teeth line the inner surfaces of the mouth and give the bass a good grip on its victim.

Bass are not colorful fish—their back is usually dull brown or green, while their underside is pale. The flanks are patterned, however, and these patterns vary according to species: the small-mouth bass has mottled vertical bars, for example, while the largemouth bass has a single horizontal stripe.

HABITAT AND DISTRIBUTION

The largemouth bass is the biggest species, weighing up to 25 pounds (11 kg). It prefers warm water and is at home in weed-filled lakes in the eastern United States, reaching as far south as Florida. The smallmouth bass originated in the cool, clear lakes and rivers of the northern United States and Canada. Both species have been introduced to other areas by fishers and are now found all over the United States and in parts of Europe and Africa. Smaller and less popular species include the spotted bass and the Guadalupe bass.

POWERFUL PREDATORS

Bass like to stalk their victims among sunken logs and dense aquatic plants. The colors and patterns on their body blend with their surround-

◀ As you might expect from its name, the largemouth bass has a big mouth, with a strong, jutting lower jaw.

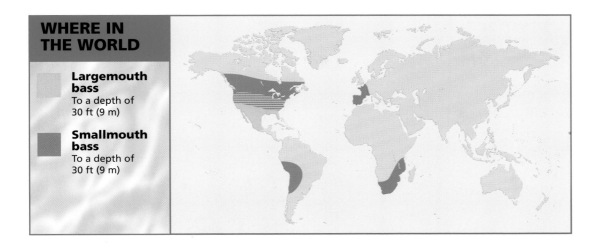

WHERE IN THE WORLD

Largemouth bass
To a depth of 30 ft (9 m)

Smallmouth bass
To a depth of 30 ft (9 m)

ings, and this camouflage helps them to get close to their prey without being detected. Their eyes, positioned on the sides of their head, give them excellent all-around vision. They are also sensitive to sounds and tastes in the water, helping them to find food in murky conditions. Young bass feed on insect larvae (young forms) and small crustaceans, but as they grow they start to tackle frogs, crayfish, and minnows. A full-grown bass feeds mainly on other fish, including smaller bass.

IN THE NEST

The male bass takes good care of his offspring. In spring or early summer he digs a hole about 12 inches (30 cm) across among logs or gravel. He chooses his nest site carefully, where there will be enough current to bring oxygen to his young without sweeping them away. The female visits the nest only briefly, laying several thousand eggs, which the male then fertilizes by covering them with his sperm. The sticky eggs attach firmly to the bottom of the nest and

hatch after about a week. Baby bass, called fry, form a shoal close to the nest and feed on plankton. The male guards them ferociously, attacking any creature that ventures too close. After about a month, when the fry are large enough to fend for themselves, they swim away. The young bass grow quickly and are able to breed after three to five years.

HUMANS AND BASS

Overfishing can reduce bass numbers, although some responsible fishers release their catch to preserve stocks. However, careless introduction of bass to areas where they are not naturally present has harmed natural ecosystems, as the predatory bass can rapidly wipe out native fish, crustaceans, and amphibians. ◆

SEE ALSO
• Fish
• Fishing
• Lake and pond
• Sunfish

▲ The smallmouth bass has a mottled pattern along its sides and a long dorsal fin that gives it stability as it swims through the water.

BEAVER

Beavers are furry mammals that dwell by streams and rivers in dense woodland. They are renowned as builders, felling trees to construct family homes called lodges.

There are only two species of beavers. The North American beaver is widespread in the United States and Canada. Its close relative, the European beaver, lives in central Europe and Mongolia. Once both species were abundant, but in past centuries millions of these creatures were killed for their valuable fur. In North America the beaver has been reestablished, but in many parts of Europe it is still scarce.

ANATOMY

Beavers are large rodents that measure up to 4 feet (122 cm) long and weigh up to 66 pounds (30 kg). The beaver's whole body is suited to its aquatic lifestyle. The powerful, webbed hind feet act as flippers, while the broad, flat tail is used mainly for steering.

Beavers have squat heads with strong jaws, small eyes, and rounded ears.

When the beaver dives, its nostrils and ears are tightly closed to prevent water from entering. A see-through eyelid also closes to protect the eye so that the beaver can see underwater.

Beavers feed on water plants and the bark, twigs, leaves, and roots of trees and shrubs. When foraging, the animal relies mainly on its keen sense of smell

▲ **This North American beaver is feeding on a willow twig in Alaska. Beavers often store twigs and branches underwater to preserve them for the winter.**

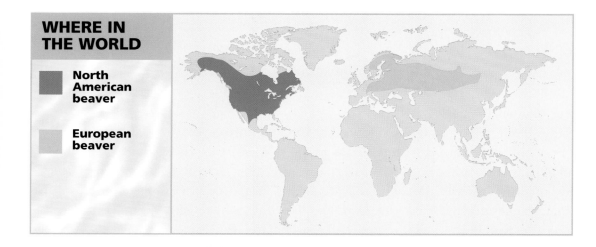

WHERE IN THE WORLD

North American beaver

European beaver

to find food, but it can also hear well, and this helps it avoid predators. The strong, sharp front teeth, or incisors, are perfect tools for gnawing through trees.

The beaver's dense brown fur is warm and waterproof. During the 18th and 19th centuries, beavers were trapped in great numbers for their pelts (skins), which were made into warm coats and hats. The fur trade was very important to the early explorers of North America, and wars were fought for control of beaver-rich country.

FAMILY LIFE

Beavers live in groups of six to ten animals: an adult male and female, their offspring from the previous year, and newborn young. Females give birth to a litter of two to four young, called kits, in spring. The babies suckle their mother's milk for six weeks, but they can swim after only a few hours. At the age of two years, the young

beavers are driven from the lodge to start their own colony.

Some beavers make their homes in riverbank burrows, but most build their lodges in midstream. Trees are felled to make a dam across the river. Water builds up behind the dam to create a lake. The lodge, made of logs, branches, rocks, and mud, is built in the middle of the lake, where predators cannot reach it. Several underwater entrances lead to a dry chamber in the center.

Over several years the beavers will enlarge their home until it becomes a sizable structure. Using their front paws, they dig canals through the surrounding land so that they can swim between pools and even float logs down to the lodge. In fall, beavers cut branches and store them underwater, ready for winter. ◆

◀ **Beavers have bright orange incisor teeth. They can gnaw through a young tree in minutes.**

FACT FILE

Name
North American beaver (*Castor canadensis*)

Habitat
Streams, lakes, and rivers in dense woodland

Food
Leaves, twigs, bark, and roots

Breeding
2–4 young (kits) born after a gestation of about 105 days

Lifespan
10–15 years

Size
32–48 in (80–122 cm) and 24–66 lb (11–30 kg)

◀ **A beaver works on its lodge. Its broad, flat tail, which acts like a rudder to steer the beaver when it is swimming, can be seen clearly.**

SEE ALSO

- Mammal
- Nutria
- Otter
- River and stream

BIOGEOGRAPHY

Biogeography is the study of the distribution patterns of plant and animal life in time and space and the factors that might explain them. To understand why an organism is present in one area but not in another requires a detailed knowledge of physical conditions, such as climate or salt levels, and biological factors, such as habitat and food availability. Past events also play an important part in determining the distribution pattern. Where did the species evolve? How has climate change influenced its survival? Are there barriers, such as expanses of dry land, that prevent it from colonizing other areas? Finding the answers to these questions is the basis of biogeography.

FACTORS AND INFLUENCES

Physical factors have an obvious effect on the distribution of organisms. For

▲ The Suez Canal cuts through the land barrier between the Mediterranean Sea (top) and Red Sea (bottom), allowing organisms to move between biogeographical regions.

▲ Coral reefs, like the one shown above, are found mostly in tropical seas because they need sunlight and warm waters to survive.

example, reef-building corals are aquatic organisms whose global distribution is strongly influenced by climate. They are found only in waters with an average temperature above 68°F (20°C). Most freshwater fish could not survive in the ocean because of the high salt levels, whereas the lack of salt in rivers and lakes would kill most marine fish. Other important physical factors include the levels of oxygen and carbon dioxide in the water, light intensity, tides, winds, and currents.

Most organisms, whatever their geographical range, require a specific type of habitat that will provide the food and other resources they need to survive. The parrot fish depends on its coral reef home for both food and shelter, and it could not survive in an area with no coral even if the water

FACT FILE

Tropical zone
A band around middle of Earth between tropic of Cancer (23° 26′ N) and tropic of Capricorn (23° 26′ S). Hot and sunny, with heavy seasonal rainfall

Temperate zones
Lie between tropics and polar regions. Neither very hot nor very cold, with limited seasonal variation

Polar regions
Antarctic Circle (about 66° 34′ S) and Arctic Circle (about 66° 34′ N). Cold to freezing temperatures; dark winter days and sunny summer nights

conditions were suitable. Areas lacking in suitable habitats act as barriers, preventing a species from spreading outside its current range.

Interactions between species have a significant influence on biogeography. For example, predators may influence the distribution of species either by preventing a prey species from becoming established in an area or by hunting local prey populations to extinction. Competition occurs when two species require the same resource, such as food or space. In some cases the resource is shared between the competitors, but in others, the better-adapted species wipes out its weaker rival.

CHANGING BARRIERS

Although all oceans are connected by the Antarctic Ocean in the Southern Hemisphere, the distribution of sea creatures is not uniform. Slow move-ments of the continents have created a changing set of barriers in the form of landmasses and deep oceans. The major barriers to species dispersal that exist today are the continents of Africa and the Americas; the huge, relatively land-less stretch of the eastern Pacific; and the deep waters of the mid-Atlantic. Freshwater habitats tend to be even more isolated from one another. As a result, different river basins and lakes with similar conditions may contain distinct fish communities.

Human activities have led to changes in biogeography. Global warming is altering the climate in many areas, and people have carelessly introduced species into places that they would not have naturally reached. Lake Victoria, once a haven for hundreds of species of cichlids, is now almost devoid of life because predatory Nile perch were introduced by fishers in the 1960s. ◆

◀ A forest of kelp (a type of seaweed) provides a complex habitat characteristic of temperate regions of the world.

BIOLUMINESCENCE

Bioluminescence is the emission of light by certain organisms. The pale green glow of fireflies fluttering through woodlands on a warm summer night is perhaps the most familiar example of bioluminescence, but this remarkable ability is far more widespread in aquatic than land creatures.

In the permanently dark waters of the ocean depths, almost every inhabitant is equipped with an elaborate set of lights. These may help them see in the gloom, hunt their prey, or even communicate with each other. For example, there are squid that dazzle their victims with powerful flashlights in their tentacles, fish with headlights that illuminate the water ahead, and shrimp that communicate by flashing complex patterns and colors to one another. The uses of bioluminescence in aquatic organisms are as diverse as the creatures themselves.

CHEMICAL LIGHT

The simplest bioluminescent life-forms are bacteria, which produce light using a chemical reaction that takes place within them. The reaction is controlled by an enzyme called luciferase and requires both oxygen and energy for it to work. (An enzyme is a type of protein that performs or regulates a chemical reaction.) This reaction is very efficient—almost all the energy is converted into light, usually yellow or

▲ An artist's representation of a deep-sea squid ejecting a cloud of glowing ink. The ink cloud distracts the predatory viper fish while the squid makes its escape.

▼ The electric organ of a hatchet-fish has a reflector and a lens, just like a flashlight does.

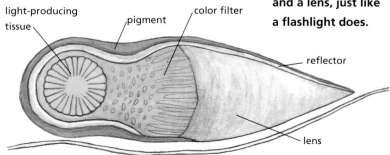

light-producing tissue

pigment

color filter

reflector

lens

green, with very little wasted as heat. This compares favorably to artificial lighting devices such as lightbulbs, which generate a lot of heat and usually convert less than 10 percent of the energy they use into light.

LIGHT ORGANS

Larger bioluminescent creatures such as fish and squid usually have light organs dotted around their bodies. In addition to light-producing tissues, these organs often contain structures such as lenses and reflectors to focus and intensify the light beam and color filters to alter the light's appearance.

Like light-producing bacteria, most of these larger animals generate light using a chemical reaction within their cells, and they can switch this reaction on and off. Some, however, cultivate colonies of bioluminescent bacteria inside their light organs. The bacteria receive oxygen and food from their host and generate light in return. The problem with this partnership is that the bacteria produce light continuously and cannot be switched off. The creatures that generate light in this way have thick membranes, similar to our eyelids, that can be drawn over their light organs to prevent light escaping.

USES OF LIGHT

Why bacteria should produce light at all is not clear. Most bioluminescent bacteria live on their own, never forming large clusters, and the light they produce is not visible to the naked eye. Some scientists think that light production is merely a side effect of a chemical pathway designed for the completely different purpose of removing oxygen. Oxygen is a very reactive element, and for organisms not able to use it, this gas can be a deadly

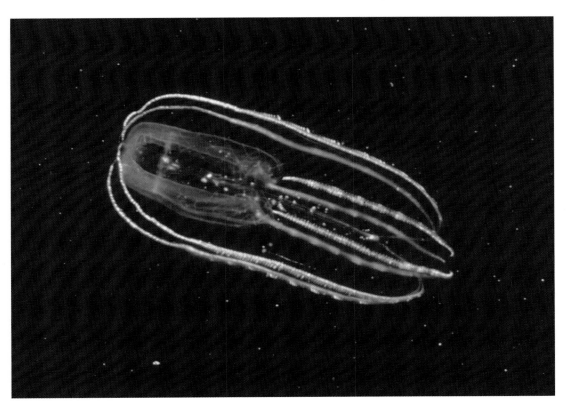

◀ **This comb jelly glows brightly with bioluminescent light as it drifts in the plankton near the surface of the sea.**

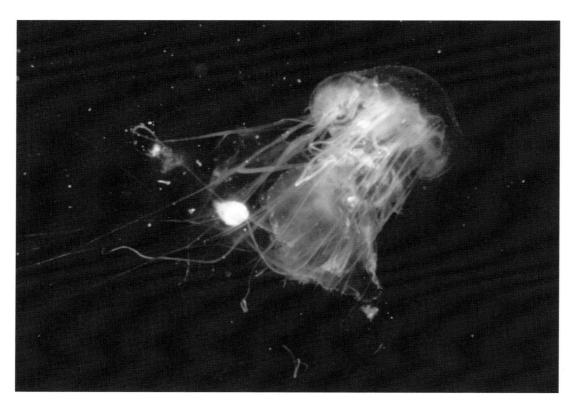

poison. Primitive bacteria first appeared at a time when there was very little oxygen in Earth's atmosphere, and as oxygen levels increased, new methods of removing it evolved. The light-producing reaction may have been one such method of consuming oxygen and preventing it from killing the bacteria.

Many creatures of the plankton, including some jellyfish and comb jellies, also use bioluminescence. Often they generate flashes of light in response to movements in the water. On certain nights, where these organisms are plentiful, they can cause the whole ocean surface to glow and sparkle. Scientists are not certain of the reasons for this behavior, but the flashes might serve to startle predators.

For larger creatures, bioluminescence has more obvious benefits. In many deep-sea animals, large light organs are present in the eye itself or just beneath it. This arrangement allows the animals to light up the water ahead and avoid predators lurking in the darkness.

Some squid and fish, such as the deep-sea hatchetfish, use their lights as a form of disguise, or camouflage. Their belly is studded with many light organs, which conceal the animals' shadow from predators swimming below and prevent them from being silhouetted against the lighter surface waters.

Other fish have bright light organs at the edges of their body and fins. These, too, are used for defense. Attackers strike at the lights and miss the main body of their target. Some squid take this strategy one step further. When threatened, they eject a cloud of glowing ink, switch off their lights, and jet away into the darkness. More often than not the predator is fooled into attacking the decoy of glowing ink, and the squid is able to escape.

Other animals use light to help them catch prey. Some deep-sea squid have bright spotlights at the end of their tentacles. They approach their targets stealthily, with their lights turned off, and release a dazzling flash at the last minute. The bright light both stuns the prey and illuminates it, giving the squid a greater chance of success.

Some animals are particularly adept at hunting with light, however. The deep-sea anglerfish has enormous jaws lined with daggerlike teeth attached to a squat body. They are not active hunters and prefer to lie in ambush for their prey. A long, glowing spine above their mouth acts like a fishing rod and attracts other fish, which may think it is something tasty to eat. When they come close enough, the anglerfish moves in and swallows them whole.

Another use of bioluminescence has been exploited by lanternfish. These small, deep-water fish like to swim in shoals, and to help them stay together, each species has a distinct pattern of light organs dotted along its flanks. Subtle differences in this pattern can be used to distinguish males from females and might be important for breeding.

HUMAN USES

Most bioluminescent creatures stop glowing shortly after death, but one small crustacean collected off the coast of Japan produces a luminous blue secretion that glows indefinitely after being dried. It can be used to decorate objects. More recently bioluminescence has become an important tool for research scientists studying the chemical reactions within cells. ◆

SEE ALSO

- Anglerfish
- Bacteria
- Comb jelly
- Deep-sea organism
- Jellyfish
- Squid

▼ A lanternfish, showing the row of bioluminescent organs along its flank. These organs help the fish keep in contact with other members of its species when swimming in shoals.

BIRD

Most people think of birds as creatures that soar high in the air on outstretched wings. Yet many types of birds are equally at home in water, and some aquatic birds, such as penguins, cannot fly at all.

Birds are found all over the world, from the tropics to the icy Arctic and Antarctica. Many species feed on land-based plants and animals; others, including ducks and grebes, live and feed in wetlands, including freshwater lakes, streams, and rivers. Of the more than 9,000 different kinds of birds, relatively few are true seabirds. The open ocean, however, is rich in food, and those birds that can survive there are often present in great numbers. Many more species of birds live at the edges of the oceans, where they make their homes on rocky cliffs, sandy beaches, salt marshes, and mudflats.

▶ **While most birds power their flight by flapping their wings, they can also use rising air currents to soar, as this herring gull is doing. Coastal and freshwater birds such as gulls and pelicans use columns of hot air called thermals to soar, mostly over the land. At sea, large birds such as albatrosses use updrafts of air caused by waves to soar.**

BODY SHAPE AND SIZE

All birds share a similar body plan, but shapes and sizes vary. Some waterbirds, such as herons and pelicans, have big, heavy bodies; others, such as freshwater dippers, are small and light. At 11 feet (3.4 m) across, the wandering albatross has the largest wingspan of any living bird. Its long wings allow it to glide efficiently over the southern oceans for months on end.

Birds' bodies are suited to their way of life and feeding habits. Ducks and swans have broad, boat-shaped bodies that balance well in water. Swans have long graceful necks for feeding underwater. Herons and many wading birds have long stiltlike legs that keep their bodies clear of the water as they stalk through the shallows.

BEAKS, FEET, AND FEATHERS

Many waterbirds, including ducks and penguins, have webbed feet that act as paddles. Others, such as grebes and

This great blue heron is hunting in a tidal pond. Its prey includes fish, small mammals, crustaceans, reptiles, birds, and insects from a variety of freshwater and brackish wetlands. The heron will stand and wait patiently, slowly stalk, or occasionally even dive to catch its prey.

coots, have toes with flattish lobes of skin that can be spread to push against the water. The freshwater jacana, or lily trotter, has long thin toes that spread the bird's weight evenly so that it can walk over soft mud or fragile lily leaves.

The legs of auks, including puffins and murres, are set far back on the body. This minimizes drag (the resistance of fluids to anything moving through them), making the birds efficient swimmers but clumsy on land. These birds do not use their feet to propel themselves when they swim; instead, they use their wings to both propel and steer them through the water.

Birds' beaks are also suited to their diets and hunting methods. Dabbling ducks have broad, flat beaks for straining weeds and tiny creatures from shallow water. Sea ducks, such as mergansers, have bills with toothed edges for grasping fish. Pelicans can store many fish at once in their pouched bills. Grebes, loons, and kingfishers have long straight bills for lunging at darting fish. Avocets and curlews have long, slim, curving bills for probing muddy shores in search of food.

All birds have feathers, which warm and protect their bodies and allow most species to fly. Below the layer of tough

A European kingfisher dives into the water to catch its prey, which will be swallowed whole.

outer feathers, wispy down feathers next to the birds' skin add extra insulation. Birds waterproof their feathers by spreading waxy oil on them with their beaks. The oil comes from a gland near their tails. The plumage of many birds blends in with their surroundings, helping them to hide from both predators and prey.

HUNTING AND FEEDING

Waterbirds feed on a wide variety of foods, from fish, crabs, and shrimp to snails, insects, and aquatic plants. They use many different methods to catch their food. Penguins, puffins, and cormorants dive deep in search of fish. Terns and gannets spot their prey from the air and plunge into the sea to make the kill. Skimmers fly just above the surface, keeping the long lower section of their beak in the water, ready to scoop up fish. Dippers search for small fish and insects in fast-flowing streams, walking along the streambed with their wings spread. Some birds hunt by day, others at dawn or dusk. Many shorebirds time their feeding with the ebb and flow of the tides.

WAYS OF LIFE

Some birds live mainly solitary lives, coming together only for breeding. Others, including oystercatchers and guillemots, are social creatures, living in flocks or loose groups for most of the year. Male and female crested grebes, swans, and gannets form pairs that remain together for life. Other birds pair up only briefly for mating and may mate with several partners in one year.

In many bird species, the bright plumage of the male attracts the female, which is often duller in color. Great

crested grebes and boobies have long and elaborate courtships and perform complicated displays to win a mate.

REPRODUCTION

All birds reproduce by laying eggs. Even birds that spend most of their lives at sea must come on land to breed. Most birds build nests to protect their eggs. The nest may be in a clump of reeds by the water's edge, in a bush or tree, on a crowded cliff ledge, or in the safety of a burrow. Birds construct their nests from

▲ A cormorant rests on a rock. Cormorants can dive to considerable depths to catch their prey, propelling themselves with their feet and balancing using their tail and wings. Some species swallow pebbles to reduce buoyancy and help them dive.

whatever materials are available: twigs and grasses, moss, seaweed, mud, or even pebbles or their own feathers.

Some birds lay many eggs at once and produce several clutches yearly. Most large seabirds lay only one egg each year. Usually it is the female that sits on the eggs to keep them warm. The eggs of some species hatch in weeks; others take months to develop.

The nestlings of land birds that nest in trees are often weak and helpless at birth. In contrast, the chicks of many waterbirds and other ground nesters are much more developed and have a protective coat of fluffy feathers. Their eyes open immediately, and they can stand and swim just hours after they are born. Many types of chicks are spotted or striped, and this camouflages them from predators.

Ducklings and some other chicks learn to fend for themselves quickly. Other young waterbirds, including albatross chicks, are fed by their parents for months before they are ready to leave the nest and fend for themselves.

MIGRATION

Many birds undertake long journeys called migrations twice a year, traveling between the safe breeding grounds they use in spring and summer and their winter feeding grounds. Some waterbirds migrate only a short distance. Other species, such as the Arctic tern and Wilson's storm petrel, cover vast distances—they fly between the Arctic and Antarctica every year.

Migrating birds are guided by Earth's magnetic fields; visual landmarks such as mountains, rivers, and the position of the Moon and stars; and some use their sense of smell. Some birds, including ducks and geese, fly in long chains or V-shaped formations, with birds taking turns flying at the tip of the V. The bird in this position expends the most energy, since it does not benefit from flying in the wake of another bird. ◆

SEE ALSO
- Duck
- Oil spill
- Penguin
- Puffin
- Tidal zone

▼ Like many other young aquatic birds, this little grebe would have been fully active from birth. Little grebes are diving, foot-propelled swimmers that can reach underwater speeds of over 6 feet (2 m) a second as adults. Baby grebes are often carried on the backs of their parents.

BLADDERWORT

◄ Many bladder-worts have slender stems topped by bright yellow flowers. The bladders are located on the underwater branches at the bottom of the plant.

Bladderworts are small plants that are common in temperate and tropical parts of the world. They live in shallow water in freshwater pools and in damp, boggy areas. Although they are widely distributed, they are little known because they are very small and easily overlooked. Bladderworts are remarkable plants, however, because they are carnivorous (meat-eating). Their stems are covered with masses of tiny traps, which they use to catch small aquatic animals such as worms and water fleas. Bladderworts have to feed in this way because they live in areas where the soil and water contain few nutrients. They need the additional nourishment if they are to grow well.

HABITATS

There are at least 250 species of bladderworts, most of which live in wetlands such as bogs. However, some are found in more unusual places, such as the small pools of water that collect in the center of epiphytes, plants that grow on tree branches high in the canopy of South American rain forests. Other rain forest bladderworts live directly on the tree branches. The very damp conditions in a rain forest provide a constant film of water in which the bladderwort's prey can swim.

▼ A bladderwort's bladder has long hairs that guide animal prey in and trigger hairs that spring the trap.

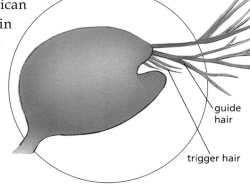

guide
hair

trigger hair

TRAPPING THEIR PREY

The traps used to capture the bladderwort's prey are tiny bladders measuring up to ⅕ inch (5 mm) in diameter, but they are usually much smaller. The traps are transparent and slightly flattened from side to side.

Each bladder is sealed by a door that opens inward. In most bladderworts there is a funnel of hairs around the entrance to the bladder. The hairs guide swimming prey into the trap. As the prey approaches the entrance, it brushes against a trigger hair, and this tiny movement causes the sides of the trap to suddenly become rounded. The drop in pressure inside the trap sucks the door open, and a current of water rushes into the bladder, carrying the prey with it. The door then springs shut, sealing the entrance and trapping the prey.

The bladderwort releases digestive juices and acid into the trap, and these kill and break down the prey's body so that its nutrients can be absorbed. Once the prey has been digested, water is gradually pumped out, flattening the bladder once again and reducing the pressure inside. About 30 minutes after capturing the meal, the trap is reset, ready for action once more.

RECOGNIZING THE BLADDERWORT

Most bladderworts consist of a tangled mass of creeping stems that float near the water's surface. Some bladderworts produce leaves that shoot straight up above the water, and several types produce flowers that look like tiny orchids. Most aquatic bladderworts die off in the winter after producing resting buds that sink to the bottom. The buds lie dormant (at rest) through the coldest months of the year, then they rise to the surface the next spring to form new plants. A few South American species live in deep water but have special floats that cause them to rise to the surface once they start developing. ◆

WHERE IN THE WORLD

■ Greater **bladderwort** To a depth of 2 ft (0.6 m)

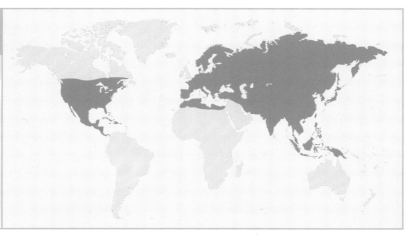

▲ Some bladderworts do not have roots, and tiny air-filled bladders keep them afloat in the water.

BLUE WHALE

The blue whale is the largest animal that has ever lived. Some of its blood vessels are the size of drainpipes, and its heart is as big as a small car. A full-grown female can measure up to 100 feet (32 m) long and weigh about 170 tons (150 metric tons): as much as 60 adult elephants or 2,500 adult humans. Males are a bit smaller, but they are still larger than any other whale.

Mighty blues are baleen whales, members of the whale family that have no teeth. Instead, hundreds of long, thin baleen plates hang down inside their mouth. Baleen is a horny, elastic material. It hangs in platelike sheets that act like sieves, filtering out the whale's food from the seawater. Blue whales feed mainly on plankton, particularly tiny shrimplike creatures such as krill, which

▲ **This blue whale has come to the surface to breathe.**

SEE ALSO

- Krill
- Mammal
- Plankton
- Whale

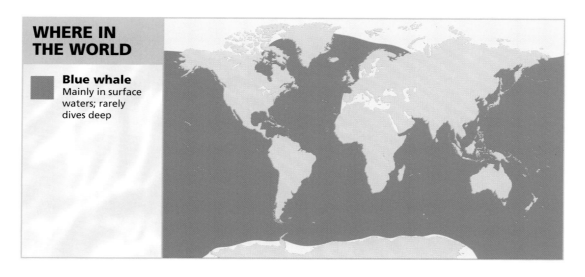

WHERE IN THE WORLD

Blue whale
Mainly in surface waters; rarely dives deep

form huge swarms in cold polar seas. The blue whale feeds at the surface and rarely dives deep.

Within the baleen whale family is a smaller group of whales called rorquals. Members of this group, including blue whales, have deep pleats in their throats and chests. These pleats allow the throat to expand, so rorquals can take in vast quantities of krill-rich seawater in a single gulp.

BODY SHAPE

The blue whale has a long, slim, dull-blue body the size of an airliner. Its rounded streamlined shape and smooth skin allow it to slip swiftly and gracefully through the water. The large tail ends in a broad, flat tail fin that sweeps up and down to power the animal forward. The smallish chest fins (flippers) help with steering. Like all rorquals, the blue whale has a small dorsal (back) fin. The tiny eyes are set deep in the head, behind the mouth. No ears are visible from the outside, though the whale can hear well. Twin blowholes on top of the head allow the animal to expel a jet of stale, steamy air and take in a fresh breath.

DISTRIBUTION

Blue whales are found in every ocean. They like to cruise in open water and are rarely seen near land.

In the summer blue whales feed in the cold waters of the Arctic and of Antarctica. In the fall they will swim thousands of miles to spend winter in the warm waters of the Tropics, where the young are born. A newborn, or calf, is the size of an elephant, measuring 23 feet (7 m) long and weighing around 2.7 tons (2.5 metric tons). The blue whale calf feeds on its mother's milk and remains at her side for many months.

Blue whales were once common throughout every ocean, particularly in southern waters. Experts estimate that 8,000 blue whales once swam in northern seas and 220,000 in southern oceans. During the 1920s and 1930s, however, commercial whalers killed huge numbers of blue whales, and by the 1960s there were only about 2,000 of these massive creatures left.

In 1966 the blue whale became officially protected as an endangered species. Populations have been slow to recover since then. Conservationists guess that only a few thousand of these gentle giants may still swim and feed in the world's great oceans. ◆

◀ The blue whale's jaw has sievelike baleen plates and long pleats that allow the whale's throat to stretch.

FACT FILE

Name
Blue whale (*Balaenoptera musculus*)

Status
Endangered

Habitat
Throughout the world's oceans, in open waters rarely near land

Food
Plankton and small fish

Breeding
Gestation 11–12 months; single calf born that matures in 6–12 years

Lifespan
60–80 years

Size
Up to 100 ft (32 m) long

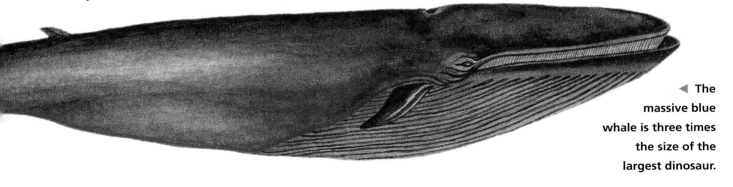

◀ The massive blue whale is three times the size of the largest dinosaur.

BRITTLE STAR

Brittle stars, and their close relatives the basket stars, are members of a large group of marine animals called echinoderms. Other members of this group include starfish, sand dollars, sea urchins, sea lilies, and sea cucumbers. Unlike most other echinoderms, brittle stars and basket stars are very active creatures, able to move rapidly and in any direction. They are sometimes called serpent stars because of the snakelike movements of their arms as they crawl across the seabed. There are about 2,000 species of brittle stars and basket stars, and they inhabit seas all around the world, from shallow water to the deepest ocean trenches.

Brittle stars have flattened, disk-shaped bodies surrounded by long flexible arms. Most species have five arms, but some have six, seven, or even nine. The disk is usually less than 1 inch (2.5 cm) across, but the arms can be quite long. The animals are often brightly colored. They tend to live alone, although some types form dense groups. They get the name of brittle star

from the ease with which the arms break off when handled, and this is probably an escape mechanism to protect the brittle star when it is attacked by a predator. Broken arms will quickly grow back.

▲ A brittle star rests on a brightly colored sponge.

FEEDING AND MOVING

Like other echinoderms, brittle stars have a complex network of narrow, water-filled passages inside their

◄ The arms of the basket star branch many times. The branches form a fine net that the animal uses to sieve food particles from the passing water currents.

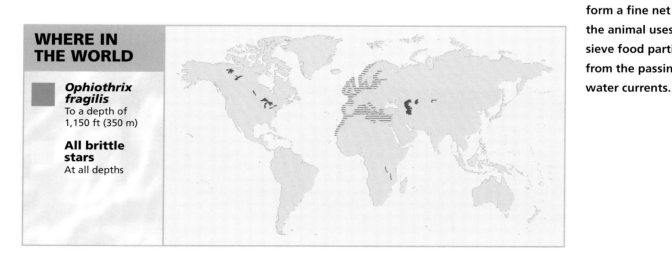

WHERE IN THE WORLD

Ophiothrix fragilis
To a depth of 1,150 ft (350 m)

All brittle stars
At all depths

bodies that connect to tiny tube feet. The feet are small hollow structures that extend when they are filled with water. As well as being organs of touch, they help the brittle star breathe. The tube feet have sticky tips and are also used to pass food particles to the mouth and keep a firm hold on the seabed.

The brittle star usually feeds on small animals and dead material that it finds in the sediment. Its mouth is on the underside of its body, and there is no anus: wastes are expelled through the mouth after the food is digested. The mouth contains a series of bony plates that grind up larger pieces of food before transporting them to the stomach to complete digestion.

BASKET STARS

Basket stars are very similar to brittle stars except that each of their arms branches several times. The branches form an intricate mesh that can be used to sieve tiny floating organisms out of the water. This animal cannot crawl as efficiently as the brittle star, so it usually positions itself on a coral or spreads itself out on some exposed area, where its arms can wave gently back and forth in the current. When disturbed, a basket star will roll itself into a tight ball.

BREEDING

Brittle stars and basket stars usually breed by shedding their eggs and sperm into the water. The fertilized eggs develop into tiny larvae (young forms) that float and feed at the surface of the ocean, forming part of the plankton. The larvae bear little resemblance to their parents, but as they grow, they change into adult form and settle on the bottom, ready to start a new life on the seabed. In a few species, fertilized eggs are kept inside the mother's body. When they emerge, the young brittle stars are tiny but fully developed. ◆

FACT FILE

Name
Ophiothrix fragilis

Distinctive features
Disklike body with five arms

Habitat
Rocky or sandy seabeds and shorelines

Food
Microscopic organisms and dead material

Breeding
Eggs and sperm are released into the water, where fertilization occurs. Young develop initially in the plankton

Lifespan
Not known

Size
Up to 12 in (30 cm) from arm tip to arm tip

◀ Where food is plentiful, brittle stars may be found in large numbers. This dense bed is in the Atlantic Ocean off Cape Hatteras, North Carolina.

SEE ALSO

- Invertebrate
- Sea lily
- Sea urchin
- Starfish

CADDIS FLY

Caddis flies are a common and wide-spread group of freshwater insects that are an important food source for fish. Many of their larvae (young stages) are easy to recognize since they protect themselves with cases made of stones, sand, or vegetation. They drag these cases with them when crawling along the bottom of streams and ponds. There are more than 10,000 known species of caddis flies in the world, including more than 1,350 in North America alone.

GROWING UP UNDERWATER

Most caddis flies have a life cycle of a year, beginning in late summer when the larvae hatch from freshly laid eggs. Many larvae then construct a case for themselves. This consists of a silk covering with stones or pieces of plant material attached to the outside. Individual species may be recognized by the kind of case they make: some are very rough and irregular, but others are built into neat shapes. The larva continues to build and alter its case as it grows. Protected inside the case, and

growing out from the abdomen (hind part) of the larva of cased species, are a series of gills. The gills and abdomen waft water through the case and out a small hole at the back, supplying the larva with oxygen as they do so.

Those larvae that build cases usually feed on fragments of dead vegetation. There are other species, however, whose larvae do

▲ A caddis fly larva crawling on underwater plants.

◄ One of the two small "legs" on the end of a caddis fly's abdomen. Each leg has a hook on the end that holds the larva inside its case.

WHERE IN THE WORLD

■ **Giant cream pattern-wing sedge** (*Hydatophylax argus*)

■ **Giant cream pattern-wing sedge** (*Hydatophylax hesperus*)

Both of the above species have the same common name

not build cases. Instead, they make silk nets of various shapes that are anchored to the bottom of streams or ponds. The nets catch tiny organisms and plant fragments, which the larvae eat. Some species build neither nets nor cases but roam free as carnivores (meat eaters). The larva of at least one New Zealand species grows up in the ocean.

TURNING INTO ADULTS

In areas with cool climates, most caddis flies spend winter as larvae. In the following spring or summer, when they have finished growing, they attach themselves to a firm anchor such as an underwater rock. Those that do not already have cases then build them for protection. After this they molt and turn into pupae, which are like the pupae of butterflies and moths but more mobile and with jaws. After two to three weeks the adult is fully developed under the pupal skin. The pupa then bites through the protective case and escapes. Sometimes with the help of air bubbles it has produced, it rises to the surface of the water, and the adult emerges from the pupal case and flies away.

Adults mainly fly at night or in twilight and look like moths. Their forewings are generally covered with hairs, giving most of them a brown appearance, although some species have patterned wings. Adults live for a few weeks or sometimes months. They cannot eat, but many can sip liquids such as nectar. After mating, the females lay eggs, either underwater or on over-hanging branches or streamside stones.

LEARNING ABOUT CADDIS FLIES

Caddis flies are a favorite food of fresh-water fish, especially trout. A lot of knowledge about the habits of caddis flies has come from fishers, and many of the artificial flies they use to catch fish are designed to look like caddis flies. More recently, caddis flies have become an important indicator of whether a stream is becoming polluted. There is still a lot to learn about these insects, however, and there may be thousands of species not yet known. ◆

FACT FILE

Name
Giant cream pattern-wing sedge (*Hydatophylax argus*)

Distinctive features
Wings patterned with cream and brown lines and spots

Habitat
Cool streams

Food
Woody debris (larvae)

Breeding
Females lay eggs on overhanging branches or streamside stones

Lifespan
One year

Size
Larva/adult up to 1.4 in (35 mm); larval case up to 3 in (75 mm)

◀ A caddis fly adult has mothlike wings and long thin antennae.

SEE ALSO

• Camouflage
• Insect
• Lake and pond
• River and stream
• Trout family

CAMOUFLAGE

A dark pike lurking on a shadowy riverbed, a shoal of striped mackerel swimming in a sunlit ocean, a glossy crab hiding on a pebbly seashore—all these creatures use camouflage to avoid being seen.

Camouflage is how animals blend in with their surroundings. The colors and shapes of many aquatic creatures' bodies help to conceal them in their watery world. Being camouflaged helps aquatic creatures in two main ways: it enables them to sneak up on their prey without being detected, and it reduces their risk of being spotted and attacked by a predator. Some creatures, such as large pike, have few predators, so their camouflage is mainly used for hunting. For others, such as the larvae (young forms) of many fish and crustaceans, a good disguise is a vital form of defense.

COLORATION AND BODY SHAPE

One of the most effective forms of camouflage is to be see-through—an approach used by much of the plankton that drifts at the surface of the oceans. Many planktonic creatures, such as fish larvae, are very small, but jellyfish, with their simple watery bodies, can grow to several feet across and remain almost invisible. Unfortunately, the dense

▼ Some animals blend with unusual backgrounds. This harlequin swimming crab from the waters of Indonesia is well camouflaged as it clings to the skin of a sea cucumber.

tissues of most larger or more complex organisms would always stand out in clear water, so these creatures use colors and body shapes for concealment. The nature of this camouflage is determined by the creature's usual surroundings. The pale, sandy colors and blotchy skin of the anglerfish make it look like a small algae-covered rock as it lurks on the seafloor. The leafy sea dragon, a large sea horse, is festooned with long, thin flaps of skin that look just like trailing fronds of seaweed.

Hiding in the sunlit surface waters of the great oceans requires a different color scheme. Many of the fish that live in this habitat, such as mackerel, have dark backs and pale bellies. This type of coloration, called countershading, counteracts the effect of sunlight shining from above. The mackerel's dark stripes and glinting scales copy the eddies and sparkles in the rippling water. Countershading helps to hide the fish from birds soaring in the air above and from aquatic predators lurking in the depths below.

In the black waters of the deep ocean, many fish have dark, patternless bodies or silvery skins that reflect dim gleams of light. Some deep-sea fish are able to produce their own light (a process called bioluminescence) to add to their disguises. The deep-sea hatchetfish has a line of tiny lights running along the underside of its body. These illuminate the fish's belly and thus conceal its outline from any animals below.

CAMOUFLAGE AND BEHAVIOR

To minimize the chances of being spotted, an animal not only must look like its surroundings, it must act like them. For creatures like the anglerfish that impersonate stationary objects, this involves staying very still. After choosing a suitable patch of seabed, an anglerfish may wait motionless for hours on end, ready to pounce on any careless fish that ventures too close. The pipefish must work a little harder to perfect its camouflage. This long, slender fish, a relative of the sea horse, must swim in a vertical position if it is to blend with the slim strands of seaweed among which it feeds.

Some water dwellers make their own disguises using the natural materials around them. Spider crabs pluck fronds of seaweed or living sponges with their pincers and plant them on their backs to help hide themselves. If the seaweed dies, the crab will replace it with a fresh

▲ The sargassum fish lives among floating rafts of sargassum that drift in tropical and temperate oceans. A relatively slow swimmer, it relies on its superb camouflage to avoid being spotted by predators and prey. Flaps of skin on its head and fins resemble the surrounding fronds of sargassum.

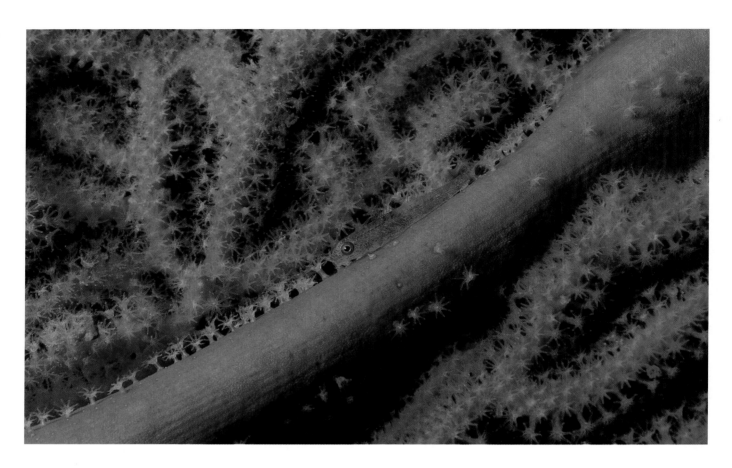

frond. In ponds and streams, caddis fly larvae spin tubes of silk around their bodies and attach small stones and weeds to create a perfect hiding place.

MASTERS OF DISGUISE

Some aquatic animals have very elaborate disguises. Bottom-dwelling flatfish such as plaice and flounder can change their body colors and patterns to blend in with different backgrounds as they move over the seabed. They can even reproduce a checkered pattern if placed on a chessboard. The pigment (color) cells in their skin occur in layers. These cells may be clumped together so that they are hidden or spread out so that they are more transparent. Only the upper surface of a plaice's body is seen as it glides over the seafloor, so only the top is camouflaged.

While flatfish take about a minute to change color, squid and cuttlefish can perform the same trick in a fraction of a second. By sending waves of color across their bodies, they can blend into moving patterns, such as ripples of sunlight sweeping across the bottom.

DISRUPTIVE PATTERNS AND WARNING COLORS

Many tropical fish have bright colors and bold patterns. Some, such as the forceps fish, have a false eye near the tail, which may fool predators into attacking the wrong end of the fish and allow it to dart away quickly. The clown fish is marked with dramatic spots and stripes that work to break up its body outline, making it hard for predators to detect. This form of camouflage is called disruptive coloration.

▲ **A tiny goby lies concealed on a brightly colored gorgonian (a type of soft coral) growing off the coast of Papua New Guinea.**

Animals that are armed with natural poisons do not use camouflage for concealment. Instead, they use bright warning colors to advertise their identity so that enemies do not try to attack them. The deadly lionfish swims openly through the water, conspicuous in its orange-and-black markings. Would-be predators recognize these warning colors and know to keep well clear. The blue-ringed octopus from the Indian and Pacific Oceans is another highly poisonous sea creature. When the octopus is threatened, bright blue ring spots appear on its skin, warning potential enemies of its deadly bite.

MIMICRY

A few creatures use a form of camouflage called mimicry to hide their true identity. Among these is the pacu, a harmless vegetarian found in the Amazon River. It is a thick-bodied fish with a red belly, making it very similar in appearance to the dangerous piranha. Enemies are fooled into thinking the pacu is a piranha and leave it alone. The false cleaner wrasse uses mimicry to get a meal. It looks and acts like a true cleaner wrasse, but as soon as a fish comes to have its parasites removed, the false cleaner darts in, takes a bite out of a fin or gill, and makes its escape. ◆

FACT FILE

Camouflage
A form of disguise used by animals to avoid detection. Most animals rely on colors and patterns that blend with the surroundings. Some are able to change color or produce light to help blend in

Disruptive coloration
The use of patterns to confuse enemies

Warning colors
Many animals use bright warning colors to deter predators

Mimicry
Mimics copy the appearance of other animals to hide their identity

◀ The sharp spines on the back and fins of this lionfish contain a powerful venom. The fish's bright colors warn potential predators to look elsewhere for a meal.

SEE ALSO

- Anglerfish
- Bioluminescence
- Flatfish
- Octopus
- Scorpion fish

CARIBBEAN SEA

The parts of the Caribbean Sea that are familiar to most people are the beautiful palm-fringed beaches where turquoise water laps gently against brilliant white sand. This tranquil setting attracts thousands of tourists each year, and most are content just to relax and soak up the sunshine. Beyond the hotels, however, the Caribbean is full of surprises. In coastal waters vast coral reefs border meadows of swaying sea grass, while farther out the bottom falls away into underwater canyons several miles deep. The Caribbean can also be a violent place. In late summer fierce hurricanes sweep through the islands, destroying anything in their path, and the region's active volcanoes can either create or devastate entire islands.

Formed millions of years ago, when the continents of North and South America were brought together by movements in the Earth's crust, the modern Caribbean is bordered at its western edge by southern Mexico and Central America. To the east lie two chains of islands, the Greater and Lesser Antilles, which together form a thin barrier against the Atlantic Ocean. The shoulder of South America lies to the

FACT FILE

Name
Caribbean Sea. Named after the Carib, the historic Native American inhabitants of some of the Lesser Antilles

Climate
Generally tropical year-round: hot and sunny. Violent tropical storms and hurricanes often occur in late summer

Habitats
Mangrove swamps, coastal lagoons, sea grass beds, coral reefs

Threats
Overfishing, pollution from industry, tourist developments

◀ A satellite picture of Hurricane Mitch crossing the Caribbean on October 26, 1998. The high winds and heavy rain associated with this hurricane devastated large areas of Central America and caused at least 10,000 deaths.

south, while the western tip of Cuba marks its northernmost point.

Most of the islands of the Caribbean were formed by volcanic eruptions, and some, such as St. Lucia, are still home to active volcanoes. Like all volcanic islands, they are mountainous, and their steep slopes are often blanketed with lush tropical forest. The island of Barbados, lying about 100 miles (160 km) east of the Lesser Antilles, was formed in a more unusual way—it is a giant prehistoric coral reef that became dry land when the water level in the world's oceans fell. Its famous white sand beaches were formed by the sea grinding down the dead corals.

Ocean currents carry a steady flow of water throughout the entire Caribbean Sea. Warm water sweeps up from the coast of Brazil as the Guiana Current joins with the North Equatorial Current and enters the Caribbean between the southern islands of the Lesser Antilles. From there it travels northward to rejoin the Atlantic via the Gulf of Mexico. The nutrient levels in the Caribbean are relatively low, but because the waters are clear, corals and sea grasses flourish, providing habitats for a wide range of aquatic creatures.

HABITATS AND SPECIES

Although the Caribbean has many beautiful beaches, its most spectacular sights are found beneath the sea's surface. Around 14 percent of the world's coral reefs lie around the region's coastlines. The largest of these, the 140-mile (220-km) barrier reef system off the coast of Belize, is second in size only to Australia's Great Barrier Reef. The reefs play a vital part in maintaining local ecosystems. They protect

▲ **A fisherman holds a spiny lobster on a beach in Tobago. Spiny lobsters were once plentiful on the reefs and sea grass beds of the Caribbean. However, fishing pressure has now severely reduced populations in many areas.**

WHERE IN THE WORLD

■ **Caribbean Sea**

Area
1,063,000 sq mi
(2,754,000 sq km)

Deepest point
Cayman Trench, 25,216 ft
(7,686 m) deep

◄ **A fishing hut and boat stand on pilings in the tranquil waters of Man-of-War Bay, Tobago.**

the coasts from being battered by waves and support many species of fish and invertebrates, some of which are found nowhere else. Moray eels lurk in the coral crevices, ready to pounce on passing fish and crustaceans, while brightly colored parrot fish crunch their way through the corals themselves.

Sea grass beds, which often form around the reefs, have interesting inhabitants of their own. Shellfish such as conchs and lobsters graze across the bottom, and rare green and loggerhead sea turtles take advantage of the gentle conditions and plentiful food. The grasses help to trap drifting sediments, preventing the corals from becoming clogged and damaged.

Closer to shore are shallow lagoons and mangrove swamps, both of which also trap sediments. These are the nurseries of the Caribbean, providing a safe home for many young aquatic animals and a nesting site for birds like the scarlet ibis. They are also a last refuge for the Caribbean manatee, a gentle plant-eating marine mammal that has been hunted almost to extinction.

Life in the open surface waters is less secure. Flying fish skip across the surface as they race away from the jaws of hunting tuna, which in turn fall victim to larger fish such as sharks and blue marlin. Some safety can be found among the drifting masses of sargassum that are swept together by swirls and eddies in the ocean currents, but even here there are hidden dangers. The sargassum fish, perfectly disguised among the floating weeds, wait for small fish to venture too close.

Some ocean dwellers choose to visit the Caribbean in order to reproduce. Bluefin tuna travel from their feeding grounds off the east coast of the United States to spawn in the waters around the Bahamas. The young tuna migrate northward to complete the cycle. Humpback whales arrive in winter to give birth to their young, called calves, in the warm, shallow waters. The adults hardly feed during their stay, which may last several months, and the calves are safe from predators in the shallow waters. Female leatherbacks cover vast distances to haul themselves ashore on a few secluded beaches. It takes them a few hours to dig a nest and lay their eggs, and then they return to the sea.

RESOURCES AND THREATS

Fishing is an important activity for many Caribbean communities. In the past, small boats and traditional methods were used to fish the inshore waters, and the catch went to local markets. Today, however, an increasing number of large, sophisticated boats, equipped with sonar to find fish and efficient nets to capture them, are operating farther from shore. This level of fishing pressure threatens fish stocks and local fishers.

In recent years large oil and mineral deposits have been found in some parts of the Caribbean. These resources provide valuable income to local economies, but their exploitation is not without hazards. Large quantities of sediment get washed from mines into the sea, where they sometimes kill corals, and floating oil and tar contribute to pollution in the area.

Tourism is the biggest source of income for many Caribbean islands, but the rapid construction of hotels and marinas has destroyed many natural habits, such as mangrove swamps and lagoons. The loss of these places can have disastrous consequences for the aquatic species that depend on them as nursery areas. ◆

SEE ALSO

- Coral reef
- Fishing
- Gulf of Mexico
- Hurricane
- Island
- Manatee and dugong
- Mangrove swamp
- Sea turtle

◄ A wealth of spectacular underwater sights can be found on the coral reefs of the Caribbean. Here, a marine worm crawls over a brightly colored coral.

CARP FAMILY

Made up of more than 2,000 species, the carp family is one of the largest families of fish. Members of this group occur naturally in the rivers and lakes of North America, Europe, Asia, and Africa. Because they are edible, hardy, and easy to raise, humans have introduced carp to areas outside their original range, such as South America, Australia, and New Zealand. Carp are also kept for decorative purposes, adding color to garden ponds. The carp family includes well-known species like goldfish and minnows.

PART OF THE FAMILY

Members of the carp family are adapted to many different habitats. The largest, the mahseer, which grows to 6 feet (1.8 m) in length, inhabits large rivers in northern India and the Himalayas. Mountain streams in Sri Lanka are home to small, colorful danios, which are popular aquarium fish. European lakes hold a number of carp relatives, including roach, rudd, tench, bream, and barbel. The carp itself is thought to have originated in the warm, weed-filled rivers of southeast Europe. Today it is widespread in Europe and present in some places in the United States.

CARP CHARACTERISTICS

Several features are shared by all members of the carp family. They have no teeth in their jaws but grind food with rough plates in their throats instead. One or two pairs of short tentacles, called barbels, hang from the corners of their mouths, and their bodies are usually covered with scales. Most carp are dull green or brown and blend with their surroundings, but males sometimes develop bright patches during the breeding season.

SENSES AND COMMUNICATION

Carp are not fussy eaters and will consume algae, mollusks, crustaceans, insects, and even aquatic plants, but they rarely attack other fish. They use their senses of smell and taste to find food, sifting through the sediment with their barbels. They are also able to hear by detecting vibrations in the water. One of the main reasons for the success of the carp family is their ability to communicate with one another using chemicals. If a carp is injured or spots a predator, it sends a chemical warning to other members of its shoal, prompting them to escape.

FACT FILE

Name
Common carp
(*Cyprinus carpio*)

Habitat
Quiet pools, lakes, and slow-flowing rivers

Food
Mollusks, insect larvae, crustaceans, and aquatic plants

Breeding
Breed in groups during summer. Eggs shed on vegetation in shallow water

Lifespan
Up to 20 years

Size
Up to 39 in (1 m) long

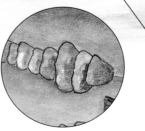

▼ Most carp have barbels, sensory tentacles used for foraging. Wild carp have scales all over their bodies. Domesticated strains, such as this mirror carp, have fewer scales.

barbel

▶ Overlapping scales provide a waterproof surface and protect the fish from scratches.

◀ **The giant danio reaches 5 inches (13 cm) in length and inhabits clean, swift-flowing streams in Sri Lanka and western India. Hardy, attractive, and peaceful, it is a popular aquarium fish.**

GROWING UP

Carp usually breed in groups. The females release their eggs over beds of aquatic plants. The sticky eggs are fertilized by sperm from the males. A large female can produce two million eggs, but carp parents make no effort to defend their young, and many are eaten by predators. The young grow quickly on a diet of plankton and algae and are soon able to tackle larger prey. Most reach maturity after three or four years.

FRIEND OR ENEMY?

Although carp are great survivors that have generally benefited from their interactions with people, their introduction into new waters in the United States and elsewhere has had unfortunate consequences for native fish. Carp stir up a lot of mud as they feed, clouding the water and killing aquatic plants. Without plants, oxygen levels in the water fall. Carp can tolerate low oxygen levels, but native fish species soon die out. Because of this, carp are considered pests in many parts of the United States, and people use nets and poisons to exterminate them. This policy has successfully eradicated carp in some waters, but they continue to thrive in others. ◆

WHERE IN THE WORLD

Common carp Includes natural distribution as well as areas to which they have been introduced

SEE ALSO

• Aquaculture
• Aquarium
• Fish
• Lake and pond

CATFISH

◀ Native to the United States, the brown bullhead can now also be found in Europe and Australia. A popular aquarium species, its introduction to new waters often results from the release of pet fish.

There are more than 2,500 species of catfish, and they are found all over the world. Many live in freshwater, though a few are found in tropical seas. They are a varied group of fish, but most have long whiskerlike structures called barbels around their mouths. The resemblance of these barbels to cat whiskers gives the group its name.

IN THE MUD

Most catfish have broad, powerful bodies with flat undersides and downward-pointing mouths—perfect for a life spent grubbing for food on the bottom. Like other fish, catfish breathe using organs called gills, but many types also use their swim bladders or intestines as lungs and can gulp air at the surface if oxygen in the water becomes scarce. Catfish do not have scales, but some are covered with interlocking armor plates. Because visibility is poor in murky water, and most catfish prefer to hunt at night, they often have poorly developed eyes and rely on other senses to find their way. Their long barbels are used to touch and taste their surroundings, while their sensitive inner ears and lateral lines can detect even slight vibrations in the water.

AROUND THE WORLD

Catfish habitats are as diverse as the creatures themselves. The mighty wels, which grows to 16 feet (5 m) long, is found in large bodies of water all over central Europe and western Asia. Lakes in North America are home to blue catfish, channel catfish, and bullheads. Small armored catfish, such as leopard corydoras, inhabit tropical pools and

FACT FILE

Name
Wels
(*Silurus glanis*)

Distinctive features
Dull brown or black above with a paler underside; blunt head and large mouth

Habitat
Large rivers and lakes. Sometimes found in estuaries

Food
Fish, frogs, crayfish, water voles, and ducklings

Breeding
Eggs are laid on vegetation in shallow water and guarded by the male

Lifespan
Not known

Size
Up to 16 ft (5 m) long

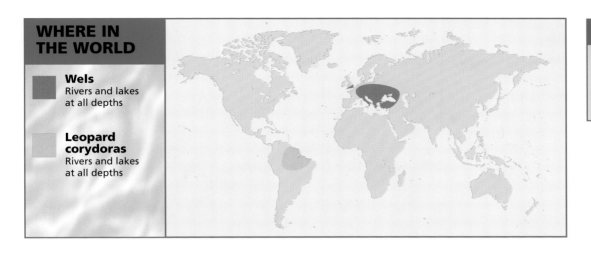

WHERE IN THE WORLD

Wels
Rivers and lakes at all depths

Leopard corydoras
Rivers and lakes at all depths

SEE ALSO

• Aquarium
• Cave
• Electric fish
• Fish

streams in South America. Air-breathing catfish, which can survive short journeys across dry land, travel between temporary pools on the African savanna. A few catfish have adapted to more specialized habitats, such as caves and deep wells.

FEEDING AND BREEDING

While the wels regularly eats ducks and rats and has even been known to attack swimming dogs, most catfish prefer smaller prey. Bottom-dwelling crustaceans and insect larvae (young forms) are favored by some, while others, such as the armored catfish, eat mainly algae. Catfish also scavenge scraps of animal and plant matter, and the smaller species are popular aquarium fish because they help to clean up debris. The tiny candirus of South America are parasites, entering the gills of other fish and sucking their blood.

Although some species are protected by poison spines, catfish rely on their senses to avoid danger. Their ability to detect chemicals in the water is particularly remarkable, enabling them to sense enemies and to communicate.

To breed, catfish release eggs into the water, where fertilization occurs. Catfish take better care of their young than most fish. Many species lay their eggs on plants in shallow water, and the parents guard them until they hatch. In most marine species the male carefully holds the young inside his mouth until they are ready to swim off. Catfish lay fewer eggs than other fish of similar size, but by taking care of them, they give their offspring a better chance of survival.

CATFISH AND PEOPLE

People fish for catfish all over the world. Some species of catfish, like the channel catfish, are caught for food, while the smaller, more colorful species are collected in large numbers for aquariums. Both these activities should be monitored closely, because they can severely reduce wild stocks. ◆

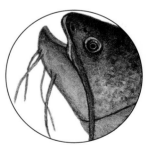

▼ **Many catfish hunt mainly at night and rely on their long barbels, which detect faint chemical traces in the water, to find food.**

◄ **The wels is a fierce predator, and there are few aquatic organisms that a full-grown specimen cannot tackle.**

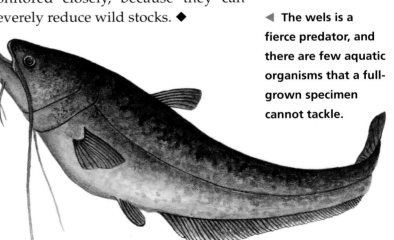

CAVE

A cave is any large underground cavity. Some are carved from rocks by waves, windblown sand, or even rain. Others are molded in volcanic lava flows. Many caves are formed when limestone is slowly dissolved by flowing water. Caves can be complex networks of twisted passages that widen into hollow caverns, where the silence is broken by water dripping into deep, clear pools. While some caves are dry inside, others are damp and dark. Most caves with access to the outside are homes for bats and other animals.

CAVE FORMATION

The largest and most complex cave systems are generally dissolved from limestone. Limestone is formed over millions of years from pieces of sea animals such as coral and the shells of other marine animals. These fragments, composed mainly of the chemical calcium carbonate, are compacted into solid rock and forced upward by movements in the Earth's crust.

Rain is slightly acidic and can dissolve calcium carbonate. When rain falls on limestone, the water seeps away through cracks and crevices, dissolving small amounts of the rock. Over thousands of years the cracks widen into smooth, water-filled passages. These underground rivers continue to carve the rocks, forming pools and waterfalls.

Each time a drop of water evaporates (turns to gas) in the cave, some of its dissolved minerals are left behind as solid crystals. Over time, these crystals form hanging spikes called stalactites on

the roof. Water drips down these spikes and collects on the floor below, where thicker mounds called stalagmites form.

CAVE DWELLERS

Deep caves have very stable climates. The temperature hardly changes with the seasons, and the air is always laden with moisture. Because there is no light, no green plants or algae can grow. Most food has to come in from outside, and it

▲ Seabirds enter the mouth of a sea cave in lava rock. Such caves provide shelter to many animals. Birds, seals, and sea lions fly or swim in, and if there is enough water, schools of fish hide in the shadows.

FACT FILE

Solution caves
Generally large caves formed as limestone or similar rocks are dissolved by flowing water. Account for the majority of caves and for the most complex systems

Lava caves
Smaller caves molded in hot, molten rock (lava) during volcanic eruptions

Glacier caves
Tunnels formed by meltwater from glacier's surface melting ice at base of glacier above bedrock

Sea caves
Hollows formed by action of waves on cracks in cliffs. The waves' pounding increases the opening until a cave is formed

is carried in either by the water or by animals such as bats that shelter inside the cave but leave it to hunt.

The decomposed bodies and droppings of bats and other cave creatures combine with sediments and run-off swept in by underground streams to nourish rafts of bacteria and fungi in the cave pools. These microorganisms form the basis of the cave food web. Specially adapted shrimp, flatworms, and other small creatures feed on these bacteria. In turn, they are preyed upon by crabs, crayfish, water beetles, salamanders, and fish.

In the darkness camouflage is unnecessary, and most cave creatures are pink or white. Many also have no eyes and rely instead on other senses to find their way. Blind salamanders and blind cave fish are able to detect vibrations in the water, while crayfish and crabs use their stalklike antennae to touch and taste their surroundings.

◄ Like other cave dwellers, blind cave fish have no eyes and are pink.

THREATS AND CONSERVATION

Caves are very fragile habitats with many unique species. As they yield their secrets to scientists and explorers, they also become more vulnerable to exploitation and damage. Souvenir hunters break off stalactites and alarm cave inhabitants. Bats will move out if they are disturbed, and without their droppings, other cave creatures can starve. To combat this threat, many cave systems are now being protected and access has been restricted. ◆

WHERE IN THE WORLD

Major cave systems

1. Mammoth Cave
(Kentucky) Longest known cave, with a surveyed length of more than 330 miles (530 km)

2. Mulu Cave (Borneo)
Perhaps the largest cave system. Only around 30 percent (120 miles; 195 km) has been surveyed

SEE ALSO

• Bacteria
• Catfish
• Coelacanth
• Crab
• Ecology
• Fish
• Salamander
• Shrimp
• Tidal zone

CHITON

Chitons (KIE-tehns), also known as coat-of-mail shells or sea cradles, are a group of mollusks commonly found in tidal zones and coastal waters around the world, although some species live at great depths. There are about 600 species of chitons, and they differ from other mollusks because they are not restricted by a rigid shell. The chiton's shell consists of eight overlapping plates embedded in the animal's mantle. The mantle extends beyond the ends of the plates to form a flexible skirt of muscle called the girdle, which protects the animal's gills. Chitons are primitive mollusks with simple digestive and nervous systems, and their fossils can be found among those of other very early forms of life.

MOVING AND FEEDING

On the underside of its body, the chiton has a large muscle called a foot. As well as gripping rock, the foot secretes a trail of slimy mucus (thick, sticky fluid). The animal crawls over this trail using a series of wavelike muscular contrac-

tions. Because the foot and the plates of the shell are flexible, the chiton is able to stick firmly to uneven surfaces. Its smooth, flattened shape makes it unlikely that it will be dislodged by the waves. If a chiton is knocked off its rock, it can roll into a ball so that the tough shell protects the soft underparts.

Most chitons feed by scraping tiny plants and animals off the rock surface with their rough tongues, called radulas. The sharp teeth on the chiton's

▲ The muscular girdle around the edge of this chiton is covered in bristles. Many chitons have bristles, spines, spicules (tiny, needle-like structures), or even scales on their girdles. These structures probably deter attack by predators and prevent barnacles and sponges settling on the chiton's girdle.

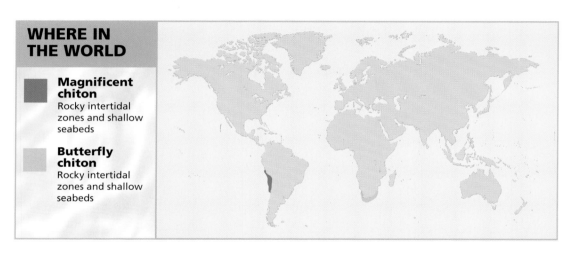

WHERE IN THE WORLD

Magnificent chiton
Rocky intertidal zones and shallow seabeds

Butterfly chiton
Rocky intertidal zones and shallow seabeds

SEE ALSO

- Invertebrate
- Mollusk
- Tidal zone

FACT FILE

Name
Gumboot chiton
(*Cryptochiton
stelleri*)

**Distinctive
features**
Unlike other
chitons, the
mantle covers
all of the shell

Habitat
Rocky intertidal
zones; shallow
waters in Pacific

Food
Algae and
other organisms
encrusting rocks

Breeding
Eggs fertilized
in female's
mantle cavity

Lifespan
Over 20 years

Size
Up to 15 in
(38 cm) long

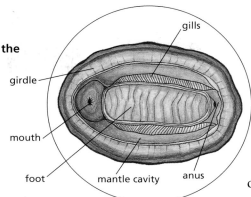

▶ This illustration of the underside of a chiton shows the mouth, anus, gills, the part of the mantle called the girdle, the mantle cavity, and the muscular foot.

radula are made of a hard mineral called magnetite, which resists wear as it scrapes the rock. A few chiton species catch larger prey, such as small shrimp. They wait with the front part of their mantles raised until likely prey wanders underneath, then clamp down to trap it.

Chitons do not have eyes, but they do have organs on the surface of their bodies that allow them to detect light. This simple sense helps them to react quickly to shadows falling over them by clamping down tightly to the surface.

HABITATS AND BREEDING

Chitons are usually found on rocky seabeds in tidal areas or in shallow water. Most chitons hide in crevices during the day, usually creeping out at night to feed. Not all chitons live in shallow water, and some are found at depths of 1,200 feet (400 m).

Most chitons are between 1 and 3 inches (2.5 to 7.5 cm) long, but some are much larger. Some chitons live for as long as 20 years, but many chitons fall victim to predators such as starfish and octopuses.

Chitons usually breed by shedding eggs or sperm into the sea. The fertilized eggs hatch into larvae (young forms) that float in the plankton at first, then settle to the seabed to complete their development. Some chitons retain their larvae inside their bodies, releasing them only when they are larger and more developed. Although this limits the number of eggs that can be produced, the young have a better chance of survival. ◆

◀ Two lined chitons graze on the organisms encrusting a rock. Unlike many chitons, the plates of the lined chiton's shell are brightly colored. Like other chitons, this species can grip the rock with its foot or clamp on to the rock with its girdle and then raise the foot to create a vacuum, which holds the chiton to the rock.

CICHLID

◄ Although they look different than most other members of the cichlid group, these graceful freshwater angelfish are cichlids. They are popular aquarium fish.

FACT FILE

Name
Convict, or zebra, cichlid (*Cichlasoma nigrofasciatum*)

Distinctive features
8–9 diagonal bars on the flanks

Habitat
Freshwater

Food
Animal and plant material

Breeding
Females spawn on the lake bed; both parents look after the eggs and young

Lifespan
Not known

Size
Up to 4 in (10 cm) long

Over 1,500 different species of cichlids (SI-kluhds) are known to science, and all are limited to freshwater or brackish environments. Most have deep, flattened bodies with fairly large fins. Some, however, such as angelfish, have disk-shaped bodies, while others, such as pike cichlids, are more elongated. Size is also variable, ranging from just over an inch (3 cm) up to 31 inches (80 cm). Their distribution is generally tropical, and they are abundant in Central and South America, Africa (including Madagascar), Israel, Syria, coastal India, and Sri Lanka.

Cichlids have a wide range of feeding habits. In the Great Lakes of central Africa, they have evolved to fill almost every position in the food web, ranging from midwater predators to grazers of algae on the lake bed. Cichlids are eaten by larger fish (including other cichlids), cormorants, and kingfishers.

Many cichlids are attractive, colorful fish, well-known and appreciated by aquarists. Several species of cichlids, known as tilapia, are produced by aquaculture and are of increasing importance as a source of food for people. The most popular of these is the Nile tilapia.

DIVERSE CREATURES

Three of the African Great Rift Valley lakes—Victoria, Malawi, and Tanganyika—house more than half the total number of cichlid species, and most of

WHERE IN THE WORLD

Convict cichlid
Shallow water

All cichlids
From shallows down to a depth of 100 ft (30 m)

SEE ALSO

- Fish
- Lake and pond

these species are found nowhere else in the world. Lake Malawi alone contains about 500 different cichlid species. This spectacular diversity is possible because of the way that cichlids feed. Unlike other fish, which usually have a rather general diet, most cichlids are specialists, adapted to exploit only one or two food sources. For example, there are species that feed on the bottom of the lake, and their diet is based on insects, algae, plant material, and small fish. Others prey on mollusks and can be divided into two groups: species that spit out the shells after eating the mollusks, and species that crush and swallow the shells. The algae eaters can also be divided. Some strain their food from the water, while others scrape it from the surface of rocks. A few large cichlids catch and eat other fish.

Some species have a more bizarre diet, including *Lipochromis*, which steals eggs and embryos from brooding female cichlids. There is also a group that eats the scales and fins of other fish.

BREEDING AND LIFE CYCLES
Cichlids have developed some interesting breeding strategies. There are two general forms of parental care: mouth-brooding and nest-building. In mouthbrooders, the female mates with more than one partner and carries the fertilized eggs and newly hatched larvae (young forms) inside her mouth. This form of care is uncommon in Central and South American cichlids, which prefer to build a nest.

Nest-building females have only one partner, and both parents guard the eggs and young. Usually the young cichlids stay in shallow water, feeding on the microscopic organisms that make up the plankton. As they grow, however, there is a change in their diet, and they move toward deeper water. Nothing is known about how long these fish live in the wild. ◆

▲ The young of this cichlid can hide from danger in their parent's mouth.

▼ This male cichlid has brightly colored spots on one of its fins. Known as egg spots, these are used to attract females during courtship and are seen only in mouthbrooding cichlid species.

CLAM

The word *clam* is commonly used to refer to a large number of soft-bodied mollusks found in many different habitats. This definition is not scientifically accurate, however, and the group includes distantly related species such as the giant clam and Pacific geoduck, as well as true clams such as quahogs and cherrystones.

Clams' closest relatives are mussels, scallops, and oysters, and like these creatures, the clam is protected by two hard shells. The shells are joined at one edge by a flexible hinge and can be closed by muscles called adductors. A clam's gills (breathing organs), mouth, and stomach are located between the shells, wrapped in a muscular structure called the mantle. Two tubes called siphons protrude from the back of the animal, while a muscle called a foot can be extended from the front.

VARIED CREATURES

Because there is little scientific basis to their grouping, the many organisms referred to as clams can seem to have

little in common with one another. Some live on mudflats or sea grass beds near the shore, but they have colonized a number of other habitats. The giant clam, a monster that can reach 4 feet (1.2 m) across, anchors itself on coral reefs in the Indian and Pacific Oceans. The small piddocks, or boring clams, live inside tunnels cut into hard substances such as rocks, concrete, or driftwood. Many clams are found in the

▲ Algae living inside the mantle give giant clams their bright colors. The algae have a place to live while providing the clams with food. This is an example of a symbiotic relationship that is beneficial to both organisms.

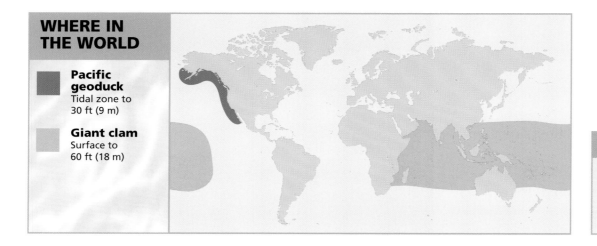

WHERE IN THE WORLD

Pacific geoduck
Tidal zone to 30 ft (9 m)

Giant clam
Surface to 60 ft (18 m)

SEE ALSO

- Aquaculture
- Mollusk
- Mussel
- Tidal zone

ocean depths. Species that are collected on mudflats around the United States include the quahog, soft-shell clam, and the geoduck, which can weigh up to 8 pounds (3.6 kg).

STAYING STILL

Clams are not fast movers. Some, like the geoduck, rarely move at all, remaining in the same spot throughout their lives. For defense they rely on their thick shells and buried lifestyle. At depths of up to 4 ft (1.2 m) beneath the mud, a geoduck can be very hard to dig out. A clam buries itself by pushing its blade-shaped foot into the sediment and then pulling its whole shell downward. The only parts of a clam that reach above the mud are the siphons. Driven by tiny hairlike structures called cilia, water flows down one siphon, across the gills, and out the other. The gills form a fine mesh that both extracts oxygen and traps food particles. The food is then transported to the mouth. At low tide, clams stop feeding and wait for the water to return.

BREEDING

Clams breed by releasing eggs or sperm into the water. There, the eggs are fertilized and develop into larvae (young forms). The larvae drift in the plankton before settling on the bottom, anchoring themselves with sticky threads and changing into adults. Many are lost to predators or swept away, but clams produce a huge number of eggs (up to one billion for giant clams), so a few are likely to survive.

HIDDEN DANGER

Clams are valuable creatures, and without protection they could easily be overexploited. In some areas wild clams can also be dangerous to eat, because their bodies concentrate poisons or pollution present in the water. Fortunately, progress is being made in raising clams using aquaculture—a safer option for clams and people. ◆

► **The water that provides a clam with food and oxygen passes down the siphon farthest from the shell hinge, across the gills, and out the other siphon.**

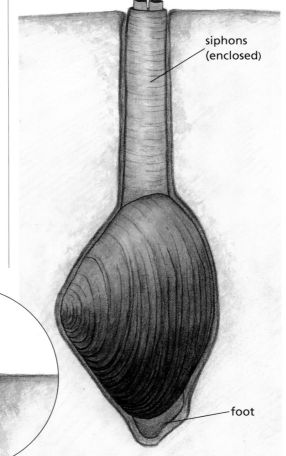

siphons (enclosed)

foot

FACT FILE

Name
Giant clam (*Tridacna gigas*)

Distinctive features
Shell valves with curved fringes; colorful mantle

Habitat
Coral reefs

Food
Filters food particles from the water and feeds on algae living inside the mantle and siphons

Breeding
Up to one billion eggs released into the water, where fertilization occurs. Larvae form part of the plankton

Lifespan
Up to 40 years

Size
Up to 4.5 ft (1.4 m) long and more than 880 lbs (400 kg)

◄ **The long siphons of the geoduck allow it to feed and breathe while safely buried several feet down in the bottom sediment. It buries itself using a blade-shaped muscular foot that can be extended from the opposite end of the shell from the siphons.**

CLINGFISH

◀ Clingfish are weak swimmers that usually rely on their excellent camouflage to avoid predators. This clingfish lives among the frondlike arms of an invertebrate called a sea lily.

FACT FILE

Name
Northern clingfish (*Gobiesox maeandricus*)

Distinctive features
Brownish gray with light and dark spots. Wide head and narrow, tapering body

Habitat
Shallow, rocky seabed and intertidal zone rock pools

Food
Small mollusks and crustaceans

Breeding
Occurs between November and May. Sticky eggs are attached under rocks. Larvae float in plankton

Lifespan
Not known

Size
Up to 6 in (15 cm) long

Clingfish are members of the Gobiesocidae (goe-bie-uh-SAHS-uh-dee) family of fish, and there are around 150 species. Most are small, well-camouflaged fish found in tropical and temperate seas and some tropical rivers and streams. Their maximum length is normally around 3 inches (7.5 cm), but different species range in size from the tiny *Derilissus nanus* at ¾ inch (1.9 cm) up to 12 inches (30 cm) for *Sicyases sanguineus*, common in coastal Chile.

Clingfish do not have scales on their bodies. Instead, they are protected by a thick coating of mucus (thick, slimy fluid). Their most obvious characteristic is a powerful sucking disk on the underside of their body. Clingfish are weak swimmers, and they spend most of their time clinging to rocks and other submerged objects. Many clingfish live in shallow waters with strong currents and wave action. They feed on limpets, chitons, and other small mollusks and crustaceans, as well as scraps carried to them by the currents. A few types of clingfish live in association with sea urchins. They seek refuge in urchins' spines and feed on their tube feet. Some tropical clingfish, such as the eastern cleaner clingfish, have been observed cleaning parasites from other larger fish.

Most clingfish are colored to resemble their surroundings, and

◀ A view of the underside of a clingfish shows its sucking disk.

WHERE IN THE WORLD

■ **Skilletfish**
Shallow seabed

■ **Northern clingfish**
Shallow seabed and intertidal zone

SEE ALSO

• Camouflage
• Fish
• Remora
• Tidal zone

some species are able to blend with many different backgrounds by changing color. These adaptations make them less visible to potential predators such as larger fish and shorebirds.

SUCKING DISK

The powerful sucking disk on the clingfish's belly is formed partly from the pelvic fins and partly from folds of skin. The disk enables the fish to attach itself to stationary objects, such as rocks, corals, or sponges, and not get washed away by water currents. The suction is so strong that a hooked clingfish can be lifted from the water along with the rock it is attached to. Clingfish almost always have flattened bodies and triangular heads. This low body profile is streamlined, reducing the chance of the fish being dragged away by a large wave or surge of current.

Clingfish are not the only fish with sucking disks on their bellies. In cool temperate and polar seas, the lumpsucker and its relative the sea snail (a fish) both have a similar adaptation. Members of the gobie family of fish, which live worldwide, also cling to rocks with modified pelvic fins.

LIFE CYCLES

The northern clingfish, a common species on the Pacific coast of California, usually breeds between November and May. Females lay rings of sticky eggs on the sheltered undersides of large rocks. On hatching, the clingfish larvae (young forms) float to the surface and drift along the coast with the plankton. The sucking disk is not present during the larval stage. The pelvic fin becomes modified into a sucking disk when the larva reaches a length of about ½ inch (13 mm). Once the disk has formed, the young clingfish sinks to the seabed and adopts an adult lifestyle. ◆

▼ A pair of clingfish rest on a sea squirt. Clingfish are able to glide across smooth objects without releasing their sucking disks.

COD FAMILY

Members of the cod family are present in great numbers in cool oceans around the world, and the large size and tasty flesh of many species make them ideal targets for fishers. Almost everyone in North America has probably eaten cod, and millions of these fish are captured each year. By studying cod, scientists hope to find ways of conserving the stocks of these valuable fish. Their research has already revealed many adaptations that have contributed to the cod family's success.

A VARIED FAMILY

The cod family is made up of more than 50 species, each preferring a particular habitat. The Arctic cod lives near the surface beneath drifting pieces of ice around the edges of the polar ice caps. Natural antifreeze in its blood allows it to withstand the freezing temperatures. Pollack and haddock are found in warmer waters around the continental shelves. Lings, the largest members of the cod family, are long, eel-like fish that are most at home close to the bottom, lurking among rocks and sunken reefs. The burbot is the only member of the cod family that lives in freshwater. It is an important predator in large, cool lakes and rivers throughout North America, Europe, and Russia. The Atlantic cod is widely distributed in the coastal waters of the northern Atlantic Ocean, where it patrols the midwaters in large shoals.

AT HOME IN THE OCEAN

Cod average between 18 and 40 inches (45 and 100 cm) in length, but they can reach 75 inches (190 cm) and weigh up to 25 lb (11 kg). Their bodies are streamlined, and this allows them to move through the water easily. They have long dorsal and anal fins. Cod are colored to blend with their surroundings. Those that live in open waters are

FACT FILE

Name
Atlantic cod
(*Gadus morhua*)

Status
Vulnerable

Habitat
Coastal waters
and open sea of
northern Atlantic

Food
Small fish
(including
herring, sprats,
and sand eels),
crustaceans,
mollusks,
and worms

Breeding
Eggs and sperm
are released into
water between
February and
April by sexually
mature fish (4–5
years old)

Lifespan
20 years

Size
Up to 75 in
(190 cm) and
25 lb (11 kg)

◀ **An Atlantic cod, commonly referred to as simply the cod, nestles in a temperate coral reef. Like other members of its species, it has a white lateral line, chin barbel, and three dorsal fins.**

silvery, while those that live among seaweed have mottled green or brown flanks that camouflage the fish. Although cod have large, sensitive eyes, little light reaches the depths at which they usually live, so they rely mainly on other senses to find food. Most cod have a barbel—a fleshy tentacle—that hangs from the lower jaw. This organ is packed with touch and taste sensors and helps the cod to detect its prey. Cod feed mainly on small fish, such as herrings, sand eels, and smaller cod, but they also eat shrimp, crabs, and mollusks.

MILLIONS OF EGGS

Between February and May cod migrate into shallow waters to breed. The male cod performs a courtship dance, bobbing and weaving before the female. Then the pair swims side by side, releasing eggs and sperm into the water. The fertilized eggs float up to the surface, where they hatch after two to four weeks. The baby cod feed on plankton, which is a mixture of tiny animals and minute plantlike organisms. Many young cod are eaten by predators, but a single adult female may produce more than six million eggs, so a few are likely to survive to maturity.

COD IN DANGER

Large numbers of cod have been captured by fishers for hundreds of years, but the cod's ability to produce enormous numbers of young has helped to ensure that populations remain stable. However, modern fishers using sonar to find shoals of cod and large, efficient nets to capture them have severely reduced cod stocks in many areas. Catch sizes are now carefully monitored to ensure that numbers recover in the future. ◆

▲ These poor cod are smaller members of the cod family, reaching an average length of 5 inches (12 cm). The favored habitats of poor cod are rocky seabeds and shipwrecks to a depth of about 1,000 feet (300 m). Poor cod prey on crustaceans and small fish.

▲ Most cod have a barbel on their chin (as here) or snout. The barbel carries microscopic taste sensors.

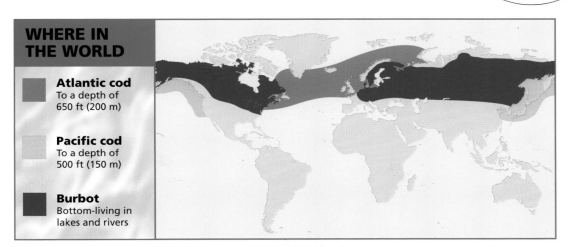

WHERE IN THE WORLD

Atlantic cod
To a depth of 650 ft (200 m)

Pacific cod
To a depth of 500 ft (150 m)

Burbot
Bottom-living in lakes and rivers

SEE ALSO
• Fish
• Fishing
• Vertebrate

COELACANTH

Coelacanths (SEE-luh-kanths) are the amazing "living fossil" fish that astonished scientists in the 1930s. They are the only living members of a large group of primitive fishes that experts at that time knew only from fossils. Fossil evidence suggests that coelacanths first appeared on Earth 350 million years ago. They were abundant and wide-spread during prehistoric times, and they colonized both fresh and salt water. However, they were believed to have died out completely around 70 million years ago, leaving lungfish as their only living relatives.

THE FISH THAT CAME BACK TO LIFE

Scientists had long written off the coelacanth as part of prehistory. Then in 1938 a fisher hauling in his catch near the port of East London, on the east coast of South Africa, discovered an unknown giant fish in his net. The first zoologist to see the specimen identified it as a coelacanth because it closely resembled the ancient fossils. Soon more coela-canths were caught off the Comoro

WHERE IN THE WORLD

Latimera chalmunae
Between 300 and 2,300 ft (100 and 700 m)

▲ A coelacanth swims in the Indian Ocean. With their strong teeth and jaws, coelacanths are efficient flesh eaters, feeding mainly on smaller fish. A joint on the skull allows the front of the head to be raised when the fish is feeding.

Islands near Mozambique. While living coelacanths had been unknown to scientists, the fish had frequently been caught by the people of the Comoro Islands. The islanders dried and salted the fish's flesh for food and used its rough, scaly skin as sandpaper to sand down old bicycle tires before repairing punctures.

The discovery that the coelacanth was not extinct caused a sensation in the scientific world because of the fish's importance in the evolution of animals with backbones (vertebrates)—a group that includes fish, reptiles, birds, and mammals. Coelacanths are related to the first fish that left the water to crawl out on land, the ancestors of modern amphibians and reptiles.

In 1998 a second species of coelacanth was discovered in Indonesia, over 5,600 miles (9,000 km) from the Comoro Islands. Little is known about this new species, and although it looks similar to its African relative, scientists believe that the two populations have been separated for at least 1.5 million years.

Modern coelacanths live in warm, tropical waters, at depths of between 300 and 2,300 feet (100 and 700 m). More than 70 specimens have now been caught and studied, and scientists have descended to the ocean floor in a submarine to study a group of six coela-canths swimming and feeding in their natural environment. During the day coelacanths hide from predators such as sharks and avoid strong currents by seeking out caves, where groups of the fish can often be found. At night they emerge to hunt smaller fish and squid.

ANATOMY

Coelacanths are large, powerful fish that measure up to 6 feet (1.8 m) long and weigh up to 200 pounds (90 kg). They have rounded blue-gray or dark brown scales and a thick, muscular tail that ends in a small lobe.

Among their most unusual features are their fleshy fins that, except for the front dorsal fin, are mounted on scaly stalks. These stalks allow the coela-canth's fins much more movement than those of other fish and bear resemblance to the limbs of more complex creatures, such as reptiles. The muscular fins on the fish's belly are thought to allow modern coelacanths to perch and rest on rocky slopes in deep water. ◆

FACT FILE

Name
Coelacanth (of Indian Ocean: *Latimeria chalumnae*)

Status
Endangered

Habitat
Rocky or coral slopes; lava caves

Food
Smaller fish; squid

Breeding
Male inserts modified fin into female to fertilize eggs, which can be tennis ball-sized. Eggs hatch inside female

Lifespan
Not known

Size
Up to 6 ft (1.8 m) long and 200 lbs (90 kg)

SEE ALSO

• Endangered species
• Fish
• Lungfish

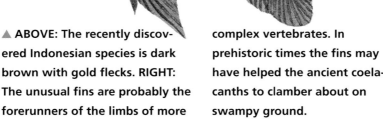

▲ **ABOVE: The recently discovered Indonesian species is dark brown with gold flecks. RIGHT: The unusual fins are probably the forerunners of the limbs of more complex vertebrates. In prehistoric times the fins may have helped the ancient coelacanths to clamber about on swampy ground.**

COMB JELLY

Comb jellies are transparent, soft-bodied animals, many of which can be found drifting slowly through cool temperate and tropical waters around the world. There are around 90 species of comb jellies all together, and their shapes vary depending on their way of life. For example, those comb jellies that live in the upper layers of the sea (such as *Pleurobrachia* species) often have rounded bodies and are sometimes called sea gooseberries or sea walnuts, while bottom-dwelling species often look like flattened worms.

Comb jellies look similar to small jellyfish, but they are not members of the animal group that contains the jellyfish. Instead, they are placed in a group of their own called the ctenophores (TE-neh-foers), meaning "comb bearers."

Comb jellies may be among the most ancient animals alive today, and although fossil remains of their delicate bodies are extremely rare, it is likely that comb jellies have lived in the oceans for hundreds of millions of years.

◄ The long feeding tentacle of a sea gooseberry has sticky threads along its length that are used to capture tiny swimming animals. Most species can retract their tentacles.

FACT FILE

Name
Sea gooseberry (*Pleurobrachia pileus*)

Habitats
Surface waters in northwest and northeast Atlantic and Black Sea

Food
Planktonic animals, especially copepods and shrimp

Breeding
Each animal has both male and female reproductive organs. Fertilization occurs outside body: eggs and sperm are shed into water

Lifespan
Not known

Size
Extended tentacles up to 12 in (30 cm) long

MOVEMENT

Comb jellies swim through the water using eight rows of hairlike structures called cilia around the edges of their bodies. The cilia in each row are joined at the base in a comblike arrangement,

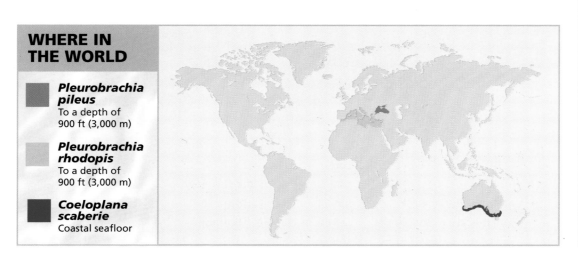

WHERE IN THE WORLD

■ *Pleurobrachia pileus*
To a depth of 900 ft (3,000 m)

Pleurobrachia rhodopis
To a depth of 900 ft (3,000 m)

■ *Coeloplana scaberie*
Coastal seafloor

giving the animal its name. The cilia beat rapidly, pushing the animal smoothly through the water. Comb jellies, however, are not strong swimmers, and their movements are largely determined by ocean currents. Sometimes they congregate in very large numbers and are driven ashore by wind or tides.

Seen underwater, a comb jelly's beating cilia produce shimmering colors like a rainbow. At night comb jellies can be even more radiant, since many types are bioluminescent (able to produce their own light). They glow brightly when the water around them is disturbed by waves, boats, or swimmers. Comb jellies are best observed while snorkeling, since their bodies are very fragile and disintegrate if they are scooped out of the water.

STICKY TENTACLES

Some of the sea gooseberries have a pair of long tentacles that they sweep through the water to locate prey such as small shrimp and newly hatched fish. Prey animals become trapped on sticky patches that line the tentacles, which then retract, pulling the victims toward the comb jelly's mouth. Other types of comb jellies have no tentacles and feed by filtering tiny creatures from a current of water that they waft over their mouths with their cilia. Still other forms have huge extendable mouths that they shoot out to engulf their prey—usually other types of comb jellies.

Comb jellies reproduce by shedding eggs or sperm into the water. The fertilized eggs hatch into larvae (young forms) that develop in the plankton. Most comb jellies take no care

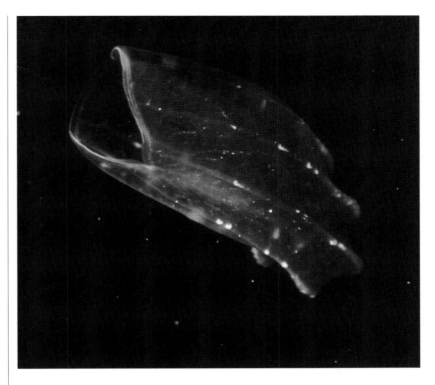

of their offspring, and the adults usually die soon after reproduction.

UNUSUAL SHAPES

As well as the more common rounded types, which are usually no more than 2 inches (5 cm) in length, there are several much larger comb jellies with unusual shapes. The Venus's-girdles, for example, are flattened, ribbon-shaped creatures, while a certain *Coeloplana* comb jelly found off the coast of Japan is flattened from top to bottom and creeps about on the seabed like a worm. ◆

▲ This bioluminescent comb jelly does not have tentacles. It feeds by drawing water in through its mouth and filtering out small particles from the plankton. The visible lines are the comb rows.

SEE ALSO
• Bioluminscence
• Digestion
• Invertebrate

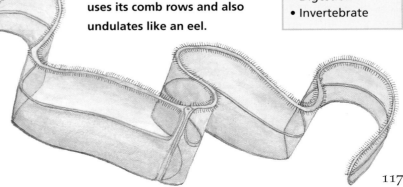

▼ To swim, this Venus's-girdle uses its comb rows and also undulates like an eel.

CONCH

◄ A queen conch, perhaps preparing to move. Conchs use the horny operculum at the base of the foot (shown here extending from the shell) to anchor into the sand. They can then use the foot as a lever to move in a series of jerks or even jumps if danger threatens. Fingerlike projections on the shell help to stabilize the animal as it moves along.

Conchs (KAHNGKS) are marine snails with heavy spiral-shaped shells. They live in shallow water in tropical seas down to a depth of about 60 feet (18 m), feeding mostly on marine algae. Their soft body parts are protected by a thick shell that often has fingerlike projections to stabilize them as they move. Conchs are most plentiful among the long strands of eelgrass that help to hide them from predators.

Like many other mollusks, the conch moves around using a large muscle called the foot. Attached to the end of a conch's foot is a hard claw-shaped plate called the operculum. The conch can dig the operculum into soft sand and use it as an anchor to help pull itself along in a series of jerks. Many conchs can bury themselves in the sand to avoid predators, but they must emerge to graze. The animal carries food to its mouth using a long tongue, or radula, which is covered with small spiny teeth.

BREEDING AND GROWTH

The most familiar type of conch is the queen conch, found throughout the Caribbean. This mollusk becomes mature after 3 years, when it weighs approximately 2 pounds (0.9 kg) and is nearly 8 inches (20 cm) long. It will continue to increase in size by 3 inches (7.5 cm) per year until its shell reaches a length of about 12 inches (30 cm) and it weighs up to 6 pounds (2.7 kg).

After mating, the female queen conch lays gel-like masses of up to half a million eggs. Tiny larvae (young forms) emerge after about five days and

FACT FILE

Name
Queen conch
(*Strombus gigas*)

Habitats
Shallow, warm seabeds and coral reefs in the Caribbean Sea

Food
Algae and moss animals

Breeding
Male and female mate, with fertilization occurring internally

Lifespan
6 to 7 years

Size
Up to 12 in (30 cm) long and up to 6 lbs (2.7 kg)

float up from the bottom to swim with the plankton as they develop. After another three weeks, the larvae are the size of a grain of sand and look like tiny snails. They sink to the seabed to continue their growth. Very few of the original half million babies survive to complete their development. Many are eaten by predators, including lobsters and sea turtles.

Some other large marine snails are often called conchs even though they do not belong to the family of true conchs, the Strombidae (STRAHM-buh-dee). Among these are such giants as the horse conch from the coast of Florida, which grows to over 2 feet (60 cm) long, and the 30-inch (77-cm) Australian trumpet, the largest marine snail.

EXPLOITING THE CONCH

The shell of the queen conch is massive. It is white on the outside and tinted a delicate pink on the inside. People have used conch shells as trumpets for thousands of years. The pointed tip is broken off and a rich sound is produced by blowing into the shell.

Conchs are good to eat, and overfishing has led to their disappearance from some areas. Shell collectors have

also taken large numbers of conchs. In the Florida Keys, conchs are now protected, but they are still imported from Caribbean islands and sold for food, so stocks continue to decline all over the region. To stay healthy, conchs need clean water that contains plenty of oxygen. Increasing pollution has reduced water quality and contributed to the reduction in conch numbers in Florida. ◆

▲ **Many conchs graze together in herds. When food gets scarce, the bed of conchs moves to another location.**

◄ **One of the movable eyestalks of a silver conch peeking out of the animal's shell. Like many conchs, this species has a slender sensory tentacle at the base of each eyestalk.**

WHERE IN THE WORLD

Rooster-tail conch
Shallow seabed down to a depth of 60 ft (18 m)

Queen conch
Shallow seabed down to a depth of 60 ft (18 m)

SEE ALSO

- Invertebrate
- Mollusk
- Snail

CONE SHELL

◀ A marbled cone shell can kill a person with its sting. Cone shell species tend to eat either worms, other mollusks, or fish. The toxins of cone shells that eat worms or mollusks are not poisonous to people. The poisons of fish-eating cone shells work equally well, however, on vertebrates other than fish, including humans.

Closely related to snails, cone shells are mollusks. They get their name from their cone-shaped shells, into which they retreat in times of danger. They are carnivores (meat eaters) that hunt other mollusks, worms, and fish. They move around using a large muscle called a foot. Those species that live on rocky seabeds glide along by passing waves of muscle contractions along this organ, while those that live on sand or mud also use the foot for burrowing. Cone shells are found in tropical and subtropical regions. They are common in the Indian and Pacific Oceans.

Cone shells find one another for mating using their senses of smell and taste. Females deposit their eggs inside

WHERE IN THE WORLD

Mediterranean cone shell
From edge of tidal zone to 400–600 ft (120–180 m) deep

Textile cone shell
From edge of tidal zone to 400–600 ft (120–180 m) deep

SEE ALSO

• Invertebrate
• Mollusk
• Snail

protective envelopes or cases strung together in gel-like ribbons. In some species the eggs hatch into larvae (young forms) that look nothing like their parents and drift in the open sea as part of the plankton. The larvae feed by straining small particles from the water through a sievelike structure. After 6 to 24 months at sea, the larvae settle on the bottom and develop into adults. Other species skip the larval stage. Their young emerge as miniature versions of the adults. Most cone shell species have a lifespan of between 4 and 16 years.

PREDATORY SNAILS

Cone shells hunt in an unusual way: they harpoon their victims with a poisoned tooth. The tooth, which forms at the end of the cone shell's tubular proboscis, is very different from those found in other snails. It is elongated and grooved with a barb on the end. A large muscular bulb at the base of the proboscis acts as an injector for a very potent poison.

Species that hunt snails can actually shoot the tooth from their proboscis like a dart, but it remains connected to the proboscis by a slender cord of tissue. Species that hunt fish or worms use their tooth like a dagger. A fish-eating cone shell lies buried in the sand and waits until a suitable target pauses above it. The fish is then speared from below and quickly injected with poison.

Cone shells usually prey on only one or two types of fish, which they detect mainly using their sense of smell. They also have simple eyes that can pick up changes in light intensity caused by the shadow of a fish swimming overhead.

DEADLY BUT BEAUTIFUL

Cone shells do occasionally sting humans, either mistaking a bather's foot for a fish or in defense when they are picked up or stepped on. Certain fish-eating species from the South Pacific are deadly to humans, and in rare cases victims have been reported to die within hours of the sting. Some cone shells are beautifully colored, and their shells are collected as ornaments or jewelry, leading to a decline in their numbers. ◆

FACT FILE

Name
Textile cone shell (*Conus textile*)

Distinctive features
Shell pattern of overlapping triangles

Habitats
Sandy, seabeds in Indian and Pacific Oceans

Food
Mollusks such as marine snails and members of its own species

Breeding
Female lays egg capsules containing more than 500 eggs on underside of rocks. Few survive to adulthood

Lifespan
Not known

Size
4–5 in (10–13 cm) long

▼ A cone shell extends its tubelike proboscis to stab a fish, which will be swallowed whole. A barbed tooth is at the end of the proboscis.

proboscis

mouth

foot

breathing siphon

▲ The cone shell takes in water through a tube called a breathing siphon. The water passes over gills, which remove the oxygen.

CONSERVATION

◄ The crescent-shaped island of Molokini, Hawaii, and its surrounding waters have been protected as a conservation area. Projects like this help protect fragile natural habitats from careless exploitation by people.

As humans evolved, water provided their basic needs, and to many it has seemed that the great waters of the world could meet human demands indefinitely. However, human populations and cities have grown so dramatically that aquatic habitats can no longer meet these demands. Food species have declined due to overfishing. Pollution presents a major threat to all forms of aquatic life. Human recreation often conflicts with the needs of wildlife, and the excessive removal of water has made some of the world's great water bodies dry up.

Conservation is the care, protection, or management of natural resources. In recent decades, society has become increasingly aware of the need to conserve natural resources of all types.

Aquatic conservation has only recently gained the attention that more traditional conservation issues have enjoyed. Urgent measures are now needed to conserve marine and freshwater environments, and conservationists are continually developing techniques to deal with demands on these resources.

CONSERVING FOOD RESOURCES

Fish and marine mammals have been among the most important food resources throughout the development of human society. The exploitation of whales and fish provided the economic incentive for the foundation of many early European settlements along the coasts of North America and elsewhere. Indeed, fisheries are still vital to the economies of many nations. However, excessive fishing pressure has driven several species to near extinction.

Several tools are now used to conserve food resources. Commercial whaling is now banned by the International Whaling Commission. However, some native peoples are allowed to continue hunting on a small scale to provide for the community's needs. Fishing quotas are now widely employed to restrict commercial catches of certain species. These can restrict catch size, the length of the fishing season, and the minimum mesh size of nets so that young fish can escape to breed. While quotas have had success in some cases, overfishing is still a problem. Once abundant species such as Atlantic cod are now classified as vulnerable (in danger of extinction in the future) by IUCN, the World Conservation Union. Even small-scale fisheries can have significant impacts on the aquatic environment. Subsistence fishers in tropical reef areas have often used dynamite to kill fish so that they can easily be collected from the surface. Such activities obviously have disastrous effects on ancient reefs and are now banned in most countries, though policing these fishing practices has proved difficult.

HUMAN THIRST FOR WATER

The great demands of human cities for water for domestic uses, including swimming pools, gardens, and golf courses, as well as for irrigation and industry, has led to the removal of great volumes of water from rivers and lakes throughout the world. At the same time, vast areas of wetlands, such as areas of the Mississippi Delta and Florida Everglades, have been drained, surrounded by levees (raised banks) to prevent flooding, and turned into

▶ A marine biologist studies the animals living on a coral reef. The captured fish will be tagged and released. Better knowledge of reef communities helps conservationists assess the threats to these areas and develop plans to preserve them.

▼ As the numbers of hotels and tourists on tropical beaches increase, safe areas for sea turtles to lay their eggs disappear. This protected beach area in Borneo is being used to incubate sea turtle eggs, a conservation activity that gives the endangered turtles a better chance of survival.

farmland. In the lower reaches of the Colorado River, physical changes in aquatic habitats have been so dramatic that they have led to the extinction of all native fish species. Similarly, the Central Valley of California was once a rich seasonal wetland that was host to hundreds of thousands of waterbirds and an important breeding ground for salmon and other fish. However, as the valley was drained to make way for agriculture, wildlife habitats have been largely lost. Local water supplies were no longer available, and the valley's farmland is now largely supplied with water drawn from neighboring states.

Prevention of the negative effects of damming, drainage, and water removal is a priority for many conservationists and has led to the development of international agreements such as the Ramsar Convention, which aims to conserve wetland habitats and their highly diverse wildlife. However, conservation is rarely the highest priority in developing hydro (water) projects, and although cases may be made for the preservation of important habitats, stronger arguments for economic development often win the debate. Cases such as that of the snail darter, a member of the perch family of fish, have drawn attention to the devastating effect of dams. No sooner was this species discovered in 1973 than its most important habitat was destroyed by the building of the Tellico Dam on the Little Tennessee River, which began in

◀ **Limestone is dumped into the headwaters of a stream in Virginia that has been polluted by acid rain. The limestone helps neutralize the acid, but the only long-term solution to acid rain, which damages freshwater habitats around the world, is to reduce levels of pollution in the atmosphere.**

1979. The dam was given the go-ahead after the federal government granted an exemption to the requirements of the Endangered Species Act. Ideally, single species protection can be an effective tool for conserving entire ecosystems. However, of all species, aquatic organisms often present the weakest political cases because of their low profile and people's poor understanding of their ecological importance.

PROTECTING AQUATIC ENVIRONMENTS FROM POLLUTION

Marine pollution incidents such as the famous wreck of the *Exxon Valdez* are headline news. These events can have catastrophic results locally and regionally. Aquatic environments are also threatened by the many more subtle effects of everyday human activities. Humans have always treated rivers and oceans as dumping grounds for their sewage. When populations were small,

this presented little problem for large water bodies, which can dilute and break down such waste. However, as cities expanded, sewage outflows exceeded the capacity of water bodies to handle the material.

More recently, humans have polluted water bodies with industrial waste, both directly and indirectly as the result of acid rain and airborne pollution. International agreements now attempt to limit releases from industry, and strict laws against pollution of waterways are in place in many industrialized nations. However, progress toward cleaning up pollutants is slow, and the effects of intense levels of pollution can be devastating. In the Great Lakes of North America, for example, sewage and industrial discharges have decimated the once important fishing industry. Even seal populations in remote areas of the Arctic Ocean have accumulated near-lethal doses of PCBs in body fat.

◄ **A biologist traps borax lake chub, which live only in Lake Borax, Oregon, and its associated marshes and ponds. Animals with limited ranges are in greater danger of habitat loss than more wide-spread organisms. These fish and their habitat are now protected by U.S. law to prevent them from becoming endangered by human activities.**

PCB (polychlorinated biphenyl) is a thick, poisonous liquid often used as an insulator in electrical equipment.

Many wetlands have been drained, but it is now known that wetland habitats can clean up polluted water bodies, and marsh grasses are being restored in many areas. The grasses use nitrogen and phosphorus from wastes such as sewage for growth. They also extract pollutants from the water. Because the reed beds slow the flow of water, sediments in the water are allowed to settle. Toxins mixed up with the sediments are then removed from circulation.

Activities such as transportation and recreation can affect the conservation value of aquatic habitats. Increasing volumes of international shipping have resulted in once silent oceans being filled with noise from marine engines. This noise is too low for human ears to detect but has been found to interfere with the social systems of whales and may affect their ability to reproduce.

Human leisure activities have also interfered with wildlife. Sea turtle breeding has been disrupted on the Greek Islands as hotels are built next to nesting areas. Coral reefs are threatened by the sheer numbers of tourists that come to experience the reefs' natural diversity of life. In many countries, marine reserves have been established to control development and pollution. However, increasing interest from tourists when an area becomes a reserve means that strict controls must be placed on recreational use.

International agreements and national plans, such as fishing quotas, marine reserves, and species protection plans, are invaluable tools for aquatic conservation. However, it is often difficult to balance the needs of wildlife with human demands for food, water, transportation, and leisure. Only by wise use of aquatic resources can humans persist on Earth, because without water, all life is threatened. ◆

SEE ALSO

- Ecology
- Endangered species
- Fishing
- Nature preserve
- Oil spill
- Pollution

GLOSSARY

amphibian: an animal that lives both on land and in water for at least part of its life

antennae: protruding "feelers" or sense organs common in invertebrates; used to touch, smell, hear, and taste the surroundings

baleen: long, stiff strips of fingernail-like material that hang from the upper jaw of certain whales; used to extract plankton in filter feeding

barbel: a fleshy filament that hangs from a fish's mouth; used to lure prey or as a sense organ

buoyancy: the force of the water surrounding a floating object that prevents it from sinking

brackish: water found in river estuaries and coastal swamps that is saltier than freshwater but less salty than seawater

camouflage: coloring or texture of an organism's exterior that makes it look like its surroundings

carnivores: animals (and a few plants) that eat other animals. **carnivorous:** adjective

cilia: tiny hairlike structures on the surface of cells used for feeding and locomotion

clutch: a collection of fertilized eggs laid at the same time by one mother

colonizing: when organisms of one or several species move into a previously unoccupied habitat

dormant: when an organism's life processes are stopped or heavily reduced until conditions become better suited for normal activity

dorsal: describing the back or top of an organism

drag: a force that acts to slow down a body as it moves through water or air

ecosystem: a community of organisms of many species that are interdependent for survival

enzyme: a protein usually used inside the body to manufacture substances needed for life

epiphyte: a type of plant that grows on other plants, using them to reach the light

fertilization: the fusion of a sperm (male sex cell) and egg (female sex cell) to produce a single cell that will grow into a unique individual

fin: limblike extensions on fish used for propulsion and steering, but also for other specializations; fish may have different numbers of fins

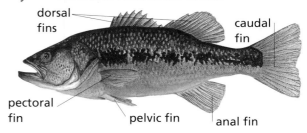

foot: the muscular part of a mollusk used mainly for movement or feeding

gills: organs used by aquatic animals to extract oxygen from water

habitat: the environment in which an organism is best suited to live

invertebrate: an animal without a backbone

larvae: young, immature animals, often very different from the adult form

mantle: the outer tissue of a mollusk from which the shell is secreted and to which it is attached

operculum: gill slit out of which water that has passed through the gills flows

parasite: an organism that is hosted by an organism of another species and harms that host

plankton: organisms that float in ocean currents

proboscis: a long extendible tonguelike structure

pupa: a life-cycle stage in which a larval form turns into a very different adult form

radula: the filelike tongue of a mollusk

shoal: a group of fish

swim bladder: an organ in fish used to control the animal's buoyancy and depth

vertebrate: an animal with a backbone

INDEX

Page numbers in *italics* refer to picture captions.